This book establishes the fact that God is all that truly satisfies. Carol Noe provides a blend of the Word of God and life's personal experiences that will enrich many!

—Joyce Meyer
Joyce Meyer Ministries, Fenton, Missouri

Having related to Carol Noe as her pastor for seventeen years, I have known her to be a person of prayer and deep commitment, with a heart to seek God Himself and to walk in His will. She has sought diligently for the answers to the questions that are addressed in this book. A determination to find His way in times of pain and trial became the crucible in which the concepts for this book were formed. Being a person who dedicated her life to service in the Kingdom of God, she has wrestled with the kind of hindrances and frustrations that pose as obstacles to anyone seeking to walk God's path. As a result, Carol is able to offer insights into principles that have been tested and proven in her own life, and she shares it all from a truly satisfied heart.

—Sue Curran
Shekinah Church Ministries, Blountville, Tennessee

The Satisfied Heart

Carol G. Noe

CREATION
HOUSE
PRESS

You open

Your hand

& satisfy

every living thing

with favor.

—Psalm 145:16 AMP

THE SATISFIED HEART by Carol Noe
Published by Creation House Press
A part of Strang Communications Company
600 Rinehart Road
Lake Mary, Florida 32746
www.creationhouse.com

This book or parts thereof may not be reproduced in any form, stored in a retrieval system or transmitted in any form by any means—electronic, mechanical, photocopy, recording or otherwise—without prior written permission of the publisher, except as provided by United States of America copyright law.

Unless otherwise noted, all Scripture quotations are from the King James Version of the Bible.

Scripture quotations marked NKJV are from the New King James Version of the Bible. Copyright © 1979, 1980, 1982 by Thomas Nelson, Inc., publishers. Used by permission.

Scripture quotations marked AMP are from the Amplified Version of the Bible

Scripture quotation marked NAS are from the New American Standard version of the Bible.

Copyright © 2000 by Carol Noe
All rights reserved

Library of Congress Cataloging-in-Publication Data
Noe, Carol.
Singleness/Carol Noe.
p.   cm.
ISBN 0-88419-645-3
1. Christian life 2. Satisfaction—religious aspects—Christianity I. Title
BV4509.5.N64   1999   99-24701
248.4--dc21   CIP

01234567 *** 87654321

Printed in the United States of America

Acknowledgements

I gratefully acknowledge the precious Holy Spirit for giving such redemptive illumination to the Scriptures and empowerment to enjoy the fulfillment of divine promises.

I also acknowledge Cathy Lechner, His faithful servant, for her obedience in announcing prophetically to me that I was to write this book for English and Spanish speaking people. Without the confirmation of her prophetic word, this book would not have been written.

And I acknowledge, also, Dr. Fuchsia Pickett, my employer and friend, who has encouraged and supported me in every step of this project and has believed in me and in God's purposes for this book.

Dedication

I dedicate this book...

to the memory of my godly father, Max Elton Noe, my first pastor and favorite preacher who taught me to fear God and obey His commandments;

and to my precious mother, Eleanor Louise Noe, whose love for God from her youth has guided me and, along with her mother's love for me, is largely responsible for my continued pursuit of God.

TABLE OF CONTENTS

Foreword

What does it mean to be successful? Where do we hope to find intimacy that will satisfy? What recourse do we have for securing justice? Where can we go to find rest? These are deep cries of every human heart on its lonely, frightening journey through life.

This world system has robbed us of satisfaction because of its godless mentality regarding success, relationship, reward, and even justice. Jesus came to give us abundant life and to satisfy the deepest cry of the human heart for intimacy, peace, justice, and yes, success. Only as we discover the wonderful truths in God's Word that reveal His longing to satisfy the desire of every living thing can we have the abundant life restored to us that He intended for us.

I have had the privilege of observing Carol Noe's life for several years in her day-to-day participation as my administrative assistant. I have come to appreciate the dignity and integrity in which she walks, evidencing the rest and satisfaction

The Satisfied Heart

she possesses because of her vital relationship with her El Shaddai. I believe that her openness in sharing these eternal truths will be an encouragement to many who seek true heart satisfaction in their relationship with God.

In this volume, Carol has reached into the private coves of her human heart and spirit to bring forth ripples and waves of rich blessing that she has discovered in her life journey as she has experienced true satisfaction in her Lord. These principles, shared in the context of her personal testimony, have a wonderful power to bring the readers to grips with the deception of discontent and to release them into new realms of satisfaction.

—Dr. Fuchsia Pickett
Blountville, Tennessee

Introduction

The loving heart of God that longs to satisfy the desires of His creatures has been maligned since the beginning of time by that evil taunt, "Hath God said...?" (See Genesis 3:1.) The philosophies of the world have turned men and women's minds against their Creator, deceiving them with their false definitions of satisfaction, intimacy, success, justice and other vital needs of the human heart.

Until we understand these basic human pursuits as they are defined by Truth and personified in Jesus, we cannot hope to ever know true heart satisfaction. The Scriptures not only show us the way to experience true satisfaction, they also empower us to receive from God the heart satisfaction that all of humanity craves. Every true believer will successfully complete his own personal journey toward satisfaction as he abandons himself to believe and obey the promises God offers.

We dare not allow the world, our family, our peers, or even the church to impose on us their faulty definitions of heart sat-

The Satisfied Heart

isfaction. If we do, we will never know the rest, the peace, the reward, and the beautiful realities of relationship that God desires for us to experience.

We continue to allow God's character to be maligned to us if we do not receive the abundant life that He has promised to us. Though we may be misunderstood by those who have bought the deceptions that define life apart from God's promises, we will be able to offer them hope of finding the heart satisfaction for which they long as they witness that satisfaction demonstrated in our lives.

My journey toward heart satisfaction is not complete. But my course is set to dispel the lies that have invaded my thinking and have kept me from knowing divine satisfaction in every area of my life. It is my prayer that the divine truths shared in the following pages that have so powerfully changed my life and allowed me to walk in true satisfaction will inspire and empower the reader to greater heart satisfaction than he (or she) has ever known.

CHAPTER 1

In Search of

Satisfaction

Understanding the Source of Discontent

Vapor of vapors and futility of futilities, says the Preacher. Vapor of vapors and futility of futilities! All is vanity (emptiness, falsity and vainglory).
—Ecclesiastes 1:2, AMP

Discontented, unhappy, dissatisfied, unfulfilled—do these words describe your life? Be honest—at least with yourself. What would it take for you to be completely satisfied and content, fulfilled and happy? Is such fulfillment possible? We cannot expect to ever know true satisfaction until we find the answers to these questions.

Though I have not often openly admitted to being discontented, many times I have silently acknowledged the discontent that arose within my heart. It seems inappropriate to admit, even to close friends, that my life experience has not been as satisfying as I had hoped it would be. Such a confession seems to diminish my sense of well-being, even my relationships. Admitting it demands an evaluation, prompts a change of that "state of mind," and forces me to face what is hindering me from pursuing contentment.

The Satisfied Heart

Some braver, more honest hearts may dare to voice their personal dissatisfaction, at least with a particular area of their lives. Perhaps expressing dissatisfaction with their employment or complaining about slow room service would not raise many disapproving eyebrows. Even discussing secret disappointment in a spouse may be acceptable with a mature confidante. But for many, these deeper issues of heart dissatisfaction are rarely discussed, perhaps for good reasons. It seems safer just to keep silent about our misery of discontent.

Perhaps we fear that an open admission of our inner discontent with life would be considered a sign of weakness—or worse, of personal failure. We might earn the disapproval of peers or significant others and risk losing their respect. And for those who were raised with a strict religious background, admitting to fundamental discontent could even be considered sin. Doesn't the Bible teach that "godliness with contentment is great gain" (1 Tim. 6:6)?

There may be other reasons as well for our silent suffering. Perhaps it is a fear that voicing our dissatisfaction with life on any level of reality would make it more painful, would somehow *empower* our discontent. What if we discovered that there were no real answers to our unhappiness? That would intensify the discontent we are trying so hard to suppress.

Of course, in our fast-paced world of near-frenzied activity, where relationship priorities are eclipsed by the "personal productivity" priority, many of us simply have not cultivated relationships of trust that could sustain a discussion of such weighty issues as *heart satisfaction*. Even if we can talk openly with a spouse or friend, we may be afraid to risk damaging that relationship by discussing our feelings of discontent. Perhaps we do not feel they have answers to the problem of discontent either, based on our observation of the ways they respond to life. We are often aware of dissatisfaction in the lives of our closest friends and relatives.

Perhaps we have even concluded that discontent, while it seems to drive humanity in a never-ending search for fulfillment, cannot ultimately be conquered. We may labor under the deception that we are doomed to live with a certain measure of discontent. Unconsciously accepting this lie as fact, we reason that we will have to continually assuage the pain of an insatiable desire for contentment. And we go through life, setting one goal after another that we hope will lead us to discover true fulfillment.

DENIAL

Some more resolute souls, unwilling to suffer the pangs of continual disappointment that come from seeking contentment in the wrong places and never finding it, have resigned themselves to a quasi-comfortable existence through *denial*. They refuse to admit that there is any disquieted desire lurking within their hearts for "something more." What, on the surface, seems like a lack of initiative is really a valiant attempt to declare they want or need nothing more than what they have already. While they may appear wiser than their frenzied friends who still pursue the goal of true fulfillment, those who deny the fact of their inner discontent must live in the bondage of this awful deception. Forever they will be unable to escape the reality of their terrible compromise with the discontent.

APPARENT SATISFACTION

There are people who seem to have found satisfaction in their pursuit of life—perhaps as a corporate executive, humanitarian, skillful wage earner, successful farmer, dedicated minister, famous athlete or performer, career woman, or mother and homemaker. These enterprising individuals concentrate all their conscious thoughts on the arena of life that has become their source of contentment, nurturing its rewards by lavishing all their energies on that pursuit. Their friends remark about them: "Their home is their life," or "The sun rises and sets in their children," or "They would play golf in a hurricane." Having found a measure of satisfaction in some pursuit of life, these people also suppress, perhaps unconsciously, the deeper inner cry for true heart satisfaction.

17

The Satisfied Heart

Sadly, though many who appear satisfied with life may succeed for years in overpowering their innate inner voice of discontent, a traumatic change in life's circumstances brings them to an inevitable day of reckoning. It may be a natural disaster of flood or fire that destroys their home, an incurable illness, an athlete's injury, a loss of popularity, bereavement for a loved one, or something as natural as retirement from a cherished position or children leaving home. Suddenly, what they have lived for is no longer there to provide the "contentment" they enjoyed.

Too often in such tragic times of life, these people become victims of personal emotional disaster, unable to cope with circumstances beyond their control. They are unable or unwilling to redefine life without the things or persons or positions they have lost. Some may never be able to recover enough stability even to seek true heart satisfaction where it can be found.

COPING WITH DISCONTENT

Since early childhood, each of us has adopted our own ways of coping with the power of discontent. Some of us learn to escape the pain of discontent through mental fantasies in which we *imagine* we have everything that can bring contentment. The lonely child, raised without siblings, develops an imaginary playmate who is always there to keep him from being alone. The bored housewife tunes into the soap operas and fills her imagination with the "excitement" of those fictitious lives, finding relief from the mundane routine of folding the laundry one more time.

The hard-driving businessman always has one more client or contract to satisfy, one more financial goal to reach. The athlete focuses on the next game or the next season when she can reach stardom. And the minister has another sermon to prepare or another building project to oversee. Others combine work, home, and community service, filling their lives with a whirl of activity that prevents any "lag time" in which to feel

18

discontent. Still others have simply become "couch potatoes," vegetating in their minds and giving up any worthwhile pursuits through their form of escape—the virtual reality of television.

In these and literally countless other ways, we have learned to hold the ravenous wolf of discontent at bay, though it is impossible to completely silence its howling. It threatens to drive us to despair if it can discover a vulnerable place in our psyche. On through life we go, structuring our days in such a way that we manage to push discontent outside the parameters of our busy lives—or *almost*. At least we never intend to confront it directly. We have painstakingly constructed our own personal delusion of contentment, and we work relentlessly to maintain it, unwilling to challenge it in any way.

We convince ourselves that the pursuit to which we have committed our energies promises us the heart satisfaction we crave. Yet, even after reaching those goals and choking back our disappointment at the lack of satisfaction they give us, most often our recourse is to rearm ourselves with an extension or expansion of those goals. If that is not possible, we quickly turn our energies to another pursuit or relationship that promises even greater satisfaction.

VICTIMS OF DISCONTENT

The advertising industry often preys upon the universal discontent that drives men, women, and children to seek satisfaction. It uses the media as an effective (shall we say, seductive) tool to inflame our inner dissatisfaction. Million-dollar ads try to convince us that some product offers true satisfaction.

The travel agent croons, "If you have not watched the romantic moonlight shimmering on the waters of the Mediterranean while standing with your beloved on the deck of our cruise ship, *Love Spectacular,* how could you expect to know contentment?" The car manufacturer implies (at times blatantly states) that until you have driven its latest model truck, you are kidding yourself that you could ever know satisfaction. And if you have not purchased the passionate scent of the most popular French *parfum*, the man with the lovely accent chides, "You cannot hope for true personal happiness." Even the brand of toothpaste and deodorant you use and the style of blue jeans you wear determine your ultimate personal contentment, according to the ads.

While advertisers' methods work successfully to sell their products, they also reinforce the deception working in many people that contentment can be attained through possessing certain material goods or through experiencing certain emotional pleasures. Their astute observations of the motivation of people brings billions of dollars of profit to their industries, while selling the public short of what they promise.

THE SOURCE OF DISCONTENT

In this brief description of mankind's drive for satisfaction I have admittedly made everyone a victim of discontent. To validate this assumption we must accept the biblical basis for mankind's universal discontent. While I do not intend to write a theological treatise regarding the nature of man, I need to establish the original source of mankind's discontent according to the Scriptures. Only then can we identify the ultimate source of mankind's satisfaction and begin our journey to embrace its reality for ourselves.

The Bible records for us the relationship Adam and Eve enjoyed with God. He talked with them in the cool of the day as He visited the beautiful garden of Eden, where He had placed the man and woman. He gave them dominion over all the earth and instructed them in the way they should live— what they were to do and what they were not to do. They enjoyed the presence of God as they fellowshiped in unbroken communion, trust, and love with their Creator. (See Genesis 3.)

That sublime relationship was severed when this first man and woman chose to disobey one of God's simple commands. Tempted by the serpent to eat from the tree of the knowledge of good and evil—a tree from which God had commanded them not to eat—Eve was deceived and ate, giving the fruit to her husband to eat as well. As a result of their disobedience, God drove man from the garden of Eden and made him till the ground in order to eat. Mankind had exchanged divine fellowship for toil; communion with God for hard labor and fatigue; dominion over the earth for the struggle for survival. After their disobedience, Adam and Eve were no longer capable of the spiritual relationship with God for which they were created.

God had warned them that if they disobeyed His command they would die. Though they continued to live on physically, their spirits died to relationship with God. Adam and Eve endured the "cosmic aloneness" that every person born since then has known because of that separation from relationship with their Creator. The New Testament refers to our being "dead in trespasses and sins" (Eph. 2:1).

Jesus confirmed this fact of spiritual death when He told Nicodemus, "Ye must be born again," referring to a spiritual rebirth that was necessary to bring us into relationship again with the kingdom of heaven (John 3:7).

When we receive the sacrifice of Jesus' blood for the forgiveness of sin—our inborn disobedience to the authority of God—our spirits are recreated, and once again we have a capacity for spiritual communion and relationship with God, for which we were created. Only by nurturing this divine relationship to maturity can we hope to find the heart satisfaction God intends for our lives.

Mankind has fallen so far from God's original divine intent that even many born-again Christians who have *initiated* a spiritual relationship with Jesus Christ still live lives that are filled with lesser pursuits that rival their pursuit of relationship with God. Unless we learn to give our relationship with God the priority Jesus taught when He said, "Seek ye first the kingdom of God, and his righteousness," we will never know the deep heart satisfaction that Christ's sacrifice made possible for us to enjoy (Matt. 6:33).

Blaire Pascal, the seventeenth century French physicist and

philosopher wrote: "There is a God-shaped vacuum in the heart of every man which cannot be filled with any created thing, but only by God, the Creator made known through Jesus Christ."[1] Knowingly, or unknowingly, Pascal articulated the biblical understanding of mankind's universal discontent. Man was created by God to enjoy unhindered fulfillment in his relationship with his Creator. God's intent for mankind was that he would know ultimate satisfaction through intimate relationship with his Creator.

Jesus declared, "I am the way, and the truth, and the life; no one comes to the Father but through me" (John 14:6, NAS). If He is the Way—and He is—then we will have to abandon *our* ways and seek His in order to silence the fearful howling of discontent within. If He is the Truth—and He is—then if we make choices apart from Him we will open our hearts to lies and deceptions of every kind that offer us satisfaction only to disappoint us in the end. If He is life—and He is—then we must allow Him to define the way we live in order to know true contentment.

Jesus offers us a *quality* of divine life that He calls abundant life (John 10:10). It is available to us when we are willing to exchange our natural dimension of life for His divine intention for us. According to the Scriptures, relationship with Jesus Christ is the only source of true contentment. To the degree we live our lives outside of Christ, we will be discontent. We can never hope to be content as long as we live without relationship with Christ, receiving His continual revelation and unfolding of our eternal destiny.

Parents and peers, the media, our own preferences, and, unfortunately, in some cases, the church, have often given us a faulty picture of fulfillment in life. To discover true heart satisfaction we must be willing for *life* to be redefined by our Savior. Only those who embrace the *Way*—Jesus—, the *Truth*—Jesus—, and the *Life*—Jesus—, have any hope of enjoying true contentment. Opening our hearts to relationship with Jesus Christ is the basic prerequisite for our dramatic deliverance from discontent.

In Search of *Satisfaction*

Though God created the entire world for man to enjoy, mankind's satisfaction was never to be pursued apart from his continual, intimate interaction with his Creator. Jesus' sacrifice on Calvary was intended to restore to man and woman what they had lost through original sin which separated them from relationship with God. Personal relationship with Jesus Christ gives us the potential for rediscovering the heart satisfaction for which we were created. Without a personal cultivation of this divine relationship, we are doomed to a life of discontent. Without understanding the true source of our discontent, we will search endlessly for satisfaction in all the wrong places.

SATISFACTION DEFINED

To *satisfy* means "to make happy, to please, to gratify to the full." *Satisfaction* is described as "the fulfillment of a need or want, contentment, gratification." The psalmist David knew God's heart toward us when he declared: "You open Your hand and satisfy every living thing with favor" (Ps. 145:16, AMP). What a picture! The hand of God, if we can imagine it, opened toward everything that has life, with one intent: to satisfy its deepest desire. Satisfaction—fulfillment, gratification, contentment—is God's idea.

Have you considered the flaming yellow forsythia blooming in early spring to be the result of a loving God opening His hand and satisfying the desire of that living bush? Or listened to the vibrantly clear song of the mockingbird and understood that the Creator delights in their satisfaction? The darling kitten playing with a ball of yarn or the pony frisking in the meadow . . . every form of life can expect to know satisfaction because that is God's desire for it. God punctuated His creation of every living thing by declaring, "It is good" (Gen. 1–3). His desire is to *satisfy* plant life and animal life, as well as His crowning glory of creation, mankind.

Many have such a faulty image of God and the relationship He desires with us that they think they can meet their own needs better without Him. They have pictured God as the austere judge of the universe, who is angry with the wicked and too busy to be concerned with their own personal needs. Even if He were concerned, they are not sure how to communicate with Him. And they wonder if He would hear them if they talked to Him.

Yet the truth is that our loving Creator-God intended for all of creation to enjoy complete satisfaction through fulfilling the purpose for their existence. By accepting this truth and acknowledging that God loves us and desires our ultimate satisfaction, we begin a wonderful journey out of spiritual darkness into marvelous light, out of personal misery into divine contentment.

DISCOVERING PERSONAL DESTINY

King Solomon, the wisest man who ever lived, considered all the pursuits of life he could imagine. After analyzing them all he declared, "Vanity of vanities . . . all is vanity" (Eccles. 12:8). Then he said, "Let us hear the conclusion of the whole matter: Fear God, and keep his commandments: for this is the whole duty of man" (Eccles. 12:13). Solomon concluded that apart from an obedient relationship with God, all of man's pursuits were worthless.

To *fear God* means "to acknowledge our need of Him" and "to cultivate an obedient relationship with Him." After we are born again, becoming sons of God, we nurture our relationship with God by reading His Word, praying, and fellowshiping with other believers, His church. As we learn to obey His commandments we will discover His purpose for our lives. Only with that sense of personal destiny can we hope to know fulfillment in life. And only as we fulfill that divine destiny for our lives will we silence forever the inner cry of discontent.

As there are no shortcuts in the natural pursuits for temporal satisfaction, so in our spiritual pursuit of true contentment, neither are there pat formulas or easy fixes that will guarantee our immediate or even our long-term gratification. However, searching for heart satisfaction through relationship with God does result in real rewards in this life as well as for eternity. If we do not pursue a vital, personal relationship with God, we will live our lives hopelessly bound to the syndrome of discontent.

Life becomes a *terrible and wonderful adventure* as we yield wholeheartedly to the plan of God that He is faithful to reveal to us. It is *terrible* in the absolute abandonment of self that is required—our will, our plans and desires, our relationships. And it is *wonderful* in the overwhelming sense of purpose, destiny, and fulfillment that only abandonment to God brings to our lives. The enlarging of our hearts in our capacity to love, our vision of eternal realities, and the rewards of service for our King eclipse the most noble plans that self, without God, could produce.

Jesus said, "Whoever finds his [lower] life will lose it [the higher life], and whoever loses his [lower] life on My account will find it [the higher life]" (Matt 10:39, AMP). As we dare to answer Christ's claim on our lives, forsaking our ways and seeking His, we will find life according to His divine intention—abundant life, peace, joy, and satisfaction. He will draw us to Himself, and, perhaps through surprising circumstances, our adventure to wholeness and fulfillment will begin. Whether we have walked with God for years or are just beginning to know Him, He delights to reveal His heart to those who dare to surrender completely and continually to Him.

Each of us can expect to receive greater revelation of His purposes in our lives as we yield more completely to Him. After walking with God in full-time ministry for over twenty years, I found myself struggling with the heart issue of discontent. Through painful circumstances, I learned to know God in a new way that established my heart in a wonderful dimension of liberty and deep contentment in life that I did not know existed. A fresh surrender to God was the key that brought me further along my journey into heart satisfaction.

CHAPTER 2

In Search of

Solitude

Triumphing over Loneliness

Therefore, behold, I will allure her, and bring her into the wilderness, and speak comfortably unto her..
—Hosea 2:14

The key grated harshly in the door of my efficiency apartment. Somehow the sound intensified the sense of panic that gripped me. Though it was a sunny fall day, and I was simply unlocking my apartment as I had many times before, the terror I felt in that moment made it seem as if I were entering the darkness of a tomb.

No one was there to greet me. But then, there never had been before. No one even knew I was there. And in that moment, it seemed that not a person in the world cared about the mental and emotional anguish I was suffering. Overwhelmed by grief and fear triggered by life's present circumstances, it was all I could do to push the door open, walk into that empty apartment, and shut the door behind me. Unloading my armful of papers, my purse, travel cup, and sweater on the kitchen table, I threw myself into the nearest chair and began to sob uncontrollably.

A DIVINE PROCESS

I had lived my adult Christian life as an energetic, productive, single woman and had become accustomed, necessarily, to going home alone. Though it usually took a few moments to "settle into aloneness" after being in the friendly company of others, I always knew that friends were nearby if I needed them, and I was generally content with my single state. Though living alone was certainly not what I considered ideal, nor what I had planned for my life, I reasoned that few people enjoyed an ideal lifestyle by whatever definition. I had much for which to be thankful.

And I was hopeful that I would not always have to live alone. Someday my dreams would come true. A handsome prince would sweep me off my feet, and, Shazam! I would exchange aloneness for my dream utopia—family! Meanwhile, I was giving my energies to the work of the Lord as administrator of a small Christian academy, Bible teacher, music teacher, and involvement in Spanish missions.

Then it happened. One summer a pastor from New Zealand visited our church. After several occasions of fellowshiping with him with a small group of friends, he asked me privately if I would be interested in a relationship with him. Recently widowed, he was looking for a godly wife. I was impressed with his gentle ways and his powerful prayer life and consented to his request for friendship. My dream seemed to be coming true. We enjoyed several months of courtship, getting to know each other and sharing our dreams of building the kingdom of God. We spent quality time together daily, praying and seeking the will of God for our lives.

It was Thanksgiving day when he placed a diamond on my finger and officially asked me to marry him. That Christmas was one to remember—the delight of shopping for each other and enjoying my favorite season together. Surely this relationship was a dream come true.

Unfortunately, the dream turned into a nightmare as the "prince" who "swept me off my feet" decided he had made a mistake. Before he got me to the altar, he took back the diamond ring along with his promises and returned to his home, leaving me to cope with the emotional pain of shattered dreams and personal rejection. It seemed harder to face, somehow, because I had waited so long for God's promised life partner. Yet I knew I had to find the grace to forgive both my ex-fiancée and others who had influenced him in his decision.

It had been only a few months earlier, the very day my fiancée was to meet my parents who were visiting from Oregon, that Dad suffered a massive stroke that left him paralyzed and without speech. While we were grateful that he recovered his mental faculties, we missed the humor and soft speech of this godly husband and parent who had taught us all the ways of God. Dad was my first pastor and is still my favorite preacher.

My hurting heart had been wrenched again, a few months after my fiancée left, by the untimely death of my younger brother, James. Five years younger than I, James was a delightful sanguine person with a brilliant mind and wonderful wit. He was the darling of our home. My twin brother, Roger, and I made life somewhat miserable for James at times while growing up. But during our teen years, James and I became wonderful friends.

We traveled together in a youth choir, and he attended the same Bible college as I did, distinguishing himself early on by becoming the national youth director for the Pentecostal organization with which that school was affiliated. He served as associate pastor of the First Open Bible Church in the city while still a student in Bible school. There were many factors that attributed to his early demise: failure in personal business that brought rejection from his mentors in ministry, refusals of marriage from several serious girlfriends, worldly lifestyles of Christian "performers" whom James admired, along with inherited weaknesses and, of course, wrong personal choices. The devastating result was that the demon of alcoholism ended his life tragically while he was still a very young man. We feared that our father's grief over the death of his attentive and beloved youngest son would take his life as well.

I had been serving as the administrator of a small Christian academy with students from kindergarten through high school. These children and young people had filled my life with their candid affection. The teachers and staff were a strong support group of friends with common goals, and they offered caring, Christian fellowship to me daily. The seven years I had served the school were some of the happiest years of my life.

However, a few weeks before my brother's death, because of the financial struggle of the small school, I was relieved of my official position, though I chose to work voluntarily with the students as I could. Still struggling with the grief of the lost hope of marriage as well as my father's stroke and my younger brother's death, I now found myself unemployed as well, for the first time in my life.

Because as a youth I had given my life to God for ministry, it seemed now that God Himself had "unemployed" me, that He did not need me. The sting of that thought was almost unbearable. Along with the grief of losing my fiancée, my brother, and my father, my personal loss of employment only deepened my depression. I felt I had lost my way in life.

All of this unresolved emotional and mental turmoil that had broken my heart overwhelmed me that day as I entered my apartment alone. In that moment, I was fighting a solitary state of mind that was terrifying. It seemed that no one knew or cared that I was suffering such deep grief, rejection, and loss of purpose. I did not know whether I could go on living. I wasn't even sure that I wanted to.

Yet, thankfully, my deeply inbred fear of God kept me from thoughts of self-destruction. I had been cultivating a personal relationship with God since I was a little child. Through personal daily devotions, faithful church attendance, Bible school studies, and mentors who inspired me to love God above all, I had disciplined myself to "seek first the kingdom of God." When I felt the Lord call me to ministry as a youth, I responded wholeheartedly. After graduating from Bible college, I had served God in children's and youth ministry, including ministry with Spanish children and youth, for over two decades.

As a single woman, I had always enjoyed the close fellowship of peers and friends in ministry who supported me as we shared our lives in the work of God together. For the first time in my life, I was experiencing deep emotional grief from the personal losses I have described, and it seemed I would have to face it *alone*. Was it possible? I was separated from my daily contact with the teachers in the school and distanced from other friends because of the months I had devoted to developing a relationship with my fiancée. Others blamed me for the failure of that relationship, and, in my pain, I withdrew.

Could I face life every day with this broken heart that sent agonizing pain searing through my chest as though it were physical? The symptoms were so alarming that I made an appointment with my physician for a thorough exam. Nothing was wrong. The physical pain was a result of my emotional state of grief and depression.

My analytical mind questioned, *Was it even Christian to be left alone like this without emotional support from family and friends? Didn't the Bible teach that we were to love one another and encourage one another in the Lord?* I was student enough of the Word to know that it did. Many times I had read the passages that teach so clearly the interdependency of the body of Christ.

I love the analogy of the body that the apostle Paul uses to teach how the church should function. He declares that Christ is the Head and we are all the various members of Christ's body. Every joint and ligament supplies what is needed for a healthy body—Christ's church. He declares that we are all needed. No one can say to another, "I don't need you" (See 1 Corinthians 12.) But where were the joints and ligaments that I needed in my present pain? How did this terrifying aloneness fit into that comforting picture? *It must be the devil,* I concluded, *trying to destroy me.*

It would be many months, even years, before I would realize that it was not the devil but the hand of God that was heavy upon me, in my pain, to deliver me from my own destructions. He was intent on setting me free from unhealthy emotional dependency in relationships to which I had looked as a source of personal contentment. He intended to restore to me the peace and joy in my relationship with Him alone that would satisfy the deepest cry of my heart. To that end, He had initiated a painful journey that would bring me to a personal wholeness and to deep heart satisfaction.

ALONENESS: A BIBLICAL PATTERN

In our journey to become rightly related to God and to people, it is often necessary to experience a season of intense aloneness. It was for me. This is true even for those who are married and involved in parenting or leading in ministry situations that involve them in various kinds of relationships.

Most of us are aware that *aloneness* is not necessarily a result of absence of people in our lives. We have all experienced that terrible sense of aloneness that occurs when we find ourselves alone in the middle of a crowd, whether in a shopping mall or a church function. The misery of aloneness we feel at such times is perhaps a result of sensing people's lack of understanding and care for our personal needs.

But when God wants to isolate a person for His purposes, it does not matter how many people he thinks are "there for him" to give them comfort and meet his personal needs. God will arrange circumstances so that we experience aloneness in order to find the source of our true satisfaction *in Him alone*. It is His mercy that leads us along this path into a season of aloneness. If we choose to follow Him, He will sever forever our selfish human tentacles of emotional and psychological need that scream to be satisfied through temporal, sometimes unhealthy, human relationships, position, and possessions.

There is a wonderful story in the Book of Hosea that illustrates this biblical pattern of the purpose of aloneness. It is an allegory of the children of Israel, describing a harlot who went after her lovers, forgetting that she was married to God. She forgot all the wonderful gifts He had bestowed on her, and she despised her relationship with her husband, God. But God would not be denied the love He desired from her. So He went after her. He declared:

> Therefore, behold, I will hedge up thy way with thorns, and make a wall, that she shall not find her paths. And she shall follow after her lovers, but she shall not overtake them; and she shall seek them, but shall not find them. Then shall she say, I will go and return to my first husband; for then was it better with me than now.
>
> —HOSEA 2:6–7

God determined to win back His bride by luring her into the wilderness and speaking comfortably unto her there (Hos. 2:14). In that desolate place, alone without her lovers, she would turn her heart to seek her true lover. It may be humbling for us to consider ourselves harlots, especially if we have walked with God at least outwardly. But if our hearts are seeking satisfaction in something or someone other than God, we are betraying His love for us. That unfaithfulness of our hearts can legitimately be called *harlotry*.

Yet God in His intense love will use circumstances to hedge up our way and bring us into a place of desolation, not to punish us, but to restore us. This is what He promises:

> And I will give her vineyards from thence, and the valley of Achor [trouble] for a door of hope: and she shall sing there, as in the days of her youth.
>
> —HOSEA 2:15A

In her valley of trouble, God promises to renew her fruitfulness and restore her joy. He goes on to say that there He will deliver her from idolatry and will betroth her to Him forever in righteousness, judgment, lovingkindness, and mercies. He promises to make her the faithful bride she never was.

And then He gives her the greatest promise of all, the promise of eternal reward.

> And I will sow her unto me in the earth; and I will
> have mercy upon her that had not obtained mercy; and I
> will say to them which were not my people, Thou art my
> people; and they shall say, Thou art my God.
>
> —HOSEA 2:23

Becoming seed for a harvest of souls must be the greatest reward we can desire. Having our lives sown in such a way that people will come to know God is surely our highest calling. Personal destiny cannot be realized without bringing others to God, becoming a part of the harvest of the earth for which Jesus died.

God's delivering purpose in our lives will inevitably lead us into wilderness experiences. There, alone and despairing, as we look to Him He will heal our backslidings and restore our souls to the purposes and joy that He alone can give to us.

BIBLE HEROES

Biblical patterns that produce such greatness in the kingdom of God should never be ignored. Many of the great men and women in Scripture experienced a desperate time of aloneness. Their struggles are recorded for us to learn from. The better we understand them, the greater our opportunity to discover our own personal destiny in God.

Abraham was required to leave his home and country and to go into a land that he didn't even know. Though he had family with him, his was a terrible aloneness, resulting from an unprecedented revelation of God that asked him to do the seemingly ludicrous. What kind of God would require a man to leave his homeland without even telling him where he was to go? Abraham was alone also with the promise of God for a son, an heir. For twenty-five years he waited for that promise to become a reality. During that time, he interceded with God—*alone*—for his nephew Lot when God determined to judge the cities of Sodom and Gomorrah. God called Abraham *friend*. It was undoubtedly the reality of this divine friendship relationship that sustained Abraham during his years of waiting and aloneness.

In Search of *Solitude*

Perhaps Abraham's greatest test of aloneness came when God asked him to take his son of promise, Isaac, to Mount Moriah and sacrifice him. His only explanation to those who were with him was, "I and the lad will go yonder and worship" (Gen. 22:5). As Abraham prepared to complete his obedience, God revealed Himself to him as *Jehovah-Jireh*, the "God who provides." He provided a ram in the thicket on that barren mountain for the sacrifice He had asked. Abraham's fresh revelation of God came because of his absolute obedience to surrender the dearest treasure of his heart back to God.

Obedience to God is seldom done in public before the admiring eyes of people. Altars of obedience are usually built alone, many times without even the comfort of counsel from those around. Yet that private obedience, which is true worship, brings great rewards to our lives that are received openly for all to see. Jesus taught us this principle when He said,

> And when thou prayest, thou shalt not be as the hypocrites are: for they love to pray standing in the synagogues and in the corners of the streets, that they may be seen of men. Verily I say unto you, They have their reward. But thou, when thou prayest, enter into thy closet, and when thou hast shut thy door, pray to thy Father which is in secret; and thy Father which seeth in secret shall reward thee openly.
>
> —MATTHEW 6:5–6

Jacob was a man who experienced great change of heart in his times of aloneness. He found himself running away in fear from his brother, Esau, whom he had tricked and cheated out of his birthright. On several occasions Jacob received a new revelation of God and of his own destiny as he slept alone and wrestled alone in the presence of God.

It is important to understand that Jacob's revelation of God came at the cost of receiving personal revelation of his own sinful nature. The angel of the Lord required Jacob to speak his own name, which meant "cheater and supplanter." In that private admission, Jacob's character was so changed that God Himself changed Jacob's name. He chose to call him *Israel,* which means "father of nations." It is as we wait alone in the presence of God that we too will experience, as Jacob did, true self-discovery that will be life changing.

Moses discovered his destiny as God's mighty deliverer as he stood alone, watching a burning bush in the wilderness. Forty years he spent in that wilderness before God revealed to him His plan and purpose for the deliverance of the Israelites from Egypt. Alone, exiled from the refinement of pharaoh's palace where he was raised, Moses encountered the power of God in that desert which changed him into the "meekest man on earth" and formed him into God's deliverer.

Isaiah's great revelation of the throne of God came as he waited alone before God. He saw the glory of God, whose train filled the temple, and seraphim flew around Him crying "holy, holy, holy."

It was then that this prophet had a deeper self-discovery, and cried out, "Woe is me! For I am undone; because I am a man of unclean lips, and I dwell in the midst of a people of unclean lips: for mine eyes have seen the King, the LORD of hosts" (Isa. 6:5). Isaiah experienced the cleansing power of God's presence as he allowed a coal from the altar of God to be placed on his lips. Though he was already ministering as a prophet, this cleansing experience prepared him for greater fruitfulness. As God asked who would go for them, Isaiah responded, "Here am I; send me" (v. 8).

Jesus Himself was not exempt from this divinely ordained season of aloneness that God requires. He was driven by the Spirit of God into the wilderness alone to be tempted by the devil forty days and nights. It was there that His ministry was established and His anointing tested, as He won that terrible battle with Satan. He demonstrated the character of the Living Word as He used the written Word to defeat the temptations of the devil.

The apostle Peter was praying alone on the rooftop when God revealed to him His plan for the gentiles to receive the gospel as well as the Jews. Cornelius, praying alone, received a vision of an angel who instructed him to send for Peter so he might receive further revelation of the gospel. And the apostle Paul spent three years in the desert alone, where he was the first to receive divine revelation of God's eternal plan for the church.

This biblical pattern of aloneness seems to be necessary for believers who want to know God, discover their destiny, and fulfill their eternal purpose. It is necessary to bring fresh revelation to our hearts of God and ourselves, prepare us for greater fruitfulness, and to cleanse us from divided devotion and other sins of harlotry. We must never fear this season or place of aloneness, for it is there that God will become to us the satisfaction of our lives.

MY PERSONAL DISCOVERY OF SOLITUDE

On that day seven years ago, as I entered my lonely apartment and sat sobbing in a chair, I finally fell on my face on the floor beside my bed and pleaded with God to give me a "safe place," one that would bring healing to my emotional and psychological pain. Since childhood I had experienced the love of God and was motivated by a deep desire to please Him. Though I could not understand love that would allow this kind of suffering, still I turned to God as I had always done to find answers to my life situations.

He had answered me many times before when I needed direction, comfort, and even temporal blessings. It seemed natural that I should turn to Him now when I needed answers to life as I had never needed them before. As I cried myself into a state of exhaustion, pouring out my grief on that occasion and similar ones that followed, I yielded my life once again to Him. I had learned that total surrender to God, no matter what it costs, was the only place that guaranteed personal safety.

I cried with the writer of the Proverbs: "The name of the LORD is a strong tower: the righteous runneth into it, and is safe" (Prov. 18:10). And I echoed the psalmist's cry: "Uphold me that I may be safe" (Ps. 119:117, NAS). As I studied that word, *safe,* I discovered that it means "preserved, free, avenged, victorious, and delivered." What promise, what hope, what a desirable place. To be free from harm and destruction, to be preserved from the wicked purposes of the enemy, and delivered from the ravages of sin—safety was a heavenly place.

I was too honest to absolve myself from all responsibility for my present state of aloneness. I knew I was guilty of leaving my first love and seeking contentment in other places. And because of some personal choices I had made, I felt responsible for some difficulties in friendship relationships. Yet, even in my emotional distress, I knew that God could keep me safe and preserve me from despair, bitterness, and other sins that would bring ultimate defeat to my life.

I reminded myself of the words of the apostle Paul who was persuaded that nothing can separate us from the love of God—"neither death, nor life, nor angels, nor principalities, nor powers, nor things present, nor things to come, nor height, nor depth, nor any other creature" (Rom. 8:38–39). The time had come for me to personally test that declaration for myself. Somehow I had to find the comfort I so desperately needed in the love of God *alone.*

Many years earlier the Holy Spirit had given me to pray, "Lord, whatever You allow to come into my life, as long as I know it is not the hand of the devil, nor my own self-will or disobedience, nor other people's misguided will, I will submit to whatever You ask me to go through." I was still willing to pray that prayer, but I was not sure I was able to keep that promise. Would I be a victim of bitterness or resentment as were others whose lives I had witnessed? Could I endure the pain of circumstances I could not change? Would my broken heart ever heal? I did not know. I could only cling to the verses of Scripture the Holy Spirit breathed into my mind and heart daily as I studied His Word—and trust.

For weeks after that, I was awakened each morning by the brilliant song of a mockingbird outside my bedroom window. No alarm clock could have motivated me to get up and face another day of emotional pain and depression. But the insistent, ever-changing song of that little bird seemed to call me from heaven to praise my God as the bird was doing for the new day that God had given us. I am convinced that God in His love assigned that little bird to me to lift my spirit and focus my confused mind on the mercy of God.

The psalms of David became the articulation for my praise and for my cry to God for help. For over three years, I do not remember reading anything except the Book of Psalms in the Scriptures. I felt strength and healing from their message pouring into my pain and giving me courage to go on. I can now say from my heart, "This is my comfort in my affliction: for thy word hath quickened me" (Ps. 119:50).

As I read, from my painful perspective, I discovered that David experienced the presence of God in places that we would not think to find Him—places of despair, of weeping, of aloneness, of trouble, and sorrow. It seemed unreasonable that God would be found in such circumstances. Yet the psalmist declared that God was there with him. He said on one occasion, "Though I walk in the midst of trouble, thou wilt revive me" (Ps. 138:7). At another time he cried to God:

> When my spirit was overwhelmed within me, Thou didst know my path. . . . Look to the right and see; for there is no one who regards me; there is no escape for me; no one cares for my soul. I cried out to Thee, O LORD; I said, "Thou art my refuge, my portion in the land of the living."
>
> —PSALM 142:3–4, NAS

David wasn't making up pretty songs when he wrote these psalms. He was living real-life experiences and expressing the pain he suffered as well as his times of rejoicing. In recording his honest reactions to his pain and difficulties, he gave us prayers that help us to form our cry to God as we walk through our own personal difficulties. One weary day, David called on God saying:

The Satisfied Heart

> Turn to me and be gracious to me, for I am lonely and
> afflicted. The troubles of my heart are enlarged; bring
> me out of my distresses.
> —Psalm 25:16–17, NAS

For months during my season of grief and aloneness, I drove every day to a state park about ten minutes from my home. Sometimes I walked around the lake if the weather were nice. Other times I just sat in my car and drank in the beauty of God's handiwork, seeking solace in the peace of His creation. Usually I found myself crying, venting my emotional pain once more, and calling on God to deliver me from my intense aloneness.

Then for a couple of weeks my busy schedule did not permit this time of daily reflection at the park. When finally I was able to return to the lake, I was surprised to find that instead of feeling as if I were going to keep a lonely tryst with my pain, there was a sense of anticipation, almost joy, at the prospect of spending time alone at the park. When I arrived, the beauty of the lake overwhelmed me, and I felt comforted there, alone with God in that beautiful place. The loneliness I had expected to engulf me had been exchanged in some miraculous way for a quiet sense of solitude and peace that I did not dream was possible.

After months of surrendering to my place of aloneness, I began to receive fresh revelation of God's love for me and to enjoy a more satisfying relationship with Him than ever before. That deepening relationship is bringing me into more healthy relationships with the body of Christ, allowing me to find the "joints and ligaments" I need, and that need me. I remember the day I was able to say with the psalmist, "It is good for me that I was afflicted, that I may learn Thy statutes" (Ps. 119:71, NAS). Stripped of everything that had given my life meaning and value, I could only cling to what it seemed I had left—a confusing and somewhat fearful relationship with God.

During these last seven years since that awful experience of entering my apartment that day, I have traveled a spiritual

40

journey that brought me out of suffocating aloneness into a place of restful solitude; out of hopeless despair into inexplicable joy; and out of terrifying fear into indescribable peace.

Though I still live in an apartment, alone, I will never again be "alone" as I was that day seven years ago. My circumstances have not changed. I have changed, or more accurately, the love and grace of God have changed me. I did not believe it was possible for a comfortable, peaceful solitude to replace that aching loneliness of my heart. Before this painful season in my life, when I had read books that declared that *aloneness* did not equal *loneliness*, I had scoffed. In my personal experience, that is exactly what aloneness had meant—a loneliness that was suffocating and paralyzing.

Now, after a busy day at the office, I enjoy retiring to the quietness of my peaceful surroundings to reflect on my day—the tasks accomplished, the things that made me laugh, and relationship involvements. Outward circumstances have not changed as dramatically as has my inward sense of well-being. God did heal my broken heart, and is delivering me from destructive thinking patterns that magnified my aloneness. Though I still do not enjoy the "heart" relationships of friends or marriage that many think are necessary for ultimate satisfaction, my journey into God during these years has brought me to a place of contentment, serenity, and joy that I did not dream was possible to find, even in the most intimate of human relationships.

The following chapters contain insights I learned as I submitted to a season of wilderness journey—*alone*. Through learning to obey these biblical principles of God, my painful loneliness and isolation have been turned into places of comfort and an enlarged capacity of love for God, for myself, and for others.

One of my favorite authors, Lloyd Ogilvie, describes mercy as "feeling another's pain in your heart."[2] A welcome result of finding God in my personal suffering has been a genuine caring and ability to weep with those who are hurting, and a desire to point them to the source of true wholeness and satisfaction.

The Satisfied Heart

But the most wonderful fruit of my season of wilderness suffering has been finding my heavenly Bridegroom in a new way and learning to hear His voice more clearly. That thrills me more than anything on earth ever could. Watching Him turn my loneliness into solitude, I have stood in awe of the joy that bursts forth from my lips in situations that had previously been so painful for me. Stripped of all human comfort as I waited before God alone, He gave me divine comfort and supernatural grace and strength that no human relationship could ever give. He healed my broken heart and gave me a future that is filled with promise.

God's provision for my temporal needs never failed, and in time God opened doors to a whole new area of ministry involving writing that has brought me to this day when I could share in print what I have learned. Not only has God restored personal relationships that were damaged, He has also placed me in the lives of other caring people. And He has given me a satisfaction and reward in my work for Him that I had never known.

I wish I could say that the entire focus of my life is now as it should be, and that all my relationships are wonderful, and that I walk completely free from all emotional pain. I cannot. But on my journey of learning to be content in God alone, I recorded some of the lessons learned that brought me into a new dimension of victory and abundant life. I can say with the psalmist, "The lines have fallen to me in pleasant places; Indeed my heritage is beautiful to me" (Ps. 16:6, NAS). In the pages that follow, I trust you with the discoveries I have made as I candidly share from my heart to yours. And I pray they will be as powerful to your fresh revelation of God and His purposes for your life as they have been in mine.

CHAPTER 3

In Search of

Peace

Experiencing Divine Reconciliation

Peace I leave with you, my peace I give unto you: not as the world giveth, give I unto you. Let not your heart be troubled, neither let it be afraid.
—John 14:27

It was the wrong choices of Adam and Eve, as we have mentioned, that created the dilemma in which we find ourselves—the "cosmic aloneness" that drives us to find some measure of connection and satisfaction with something or someone somewhere in our relentless search for peace. Because mankind disobeyed God in the garden and lost its relationship with its Creator, every person born into the world is faced with the dilemma of separation from God. That separation is intolerable to the human psyche, which senses it is adrift, alone, exiled from its true purpose, without knowing how to find its way home. A. W. Tozer expresses this misery:

> The cause of all our human miseries is a radical moral dislocation, an upset in our relation to God and to each other. For whatever else the Fall may have been, it was certainly a sharp change in man's relation to his

Creator. He adopted toward God an altered attitude, and by so doing destroyed the proper Creator-creature relation in which, unknown to him, his true happiness lay. Essentially, salvation is the restoration of a right relation between man and his Creator, a bringing back to normal of the Creator-creature relation.[3]

MANKIND'S DILEMMA

How can we ever fathom the love of God to us, a love that would send His Son, Jesus, to become a man—God the Creator becoming a created being—to reconcile us back to Himself? His purpose in creating mankind could be realized only in having men and women live in a love relationship with Him through their personal choices. So Christ made it possible for men and women who accept the sacrifice of Jesus' blood shed for their sin—that inborn disobedience to the commands of God—to choose to be reconciled to their Savior and Creator and enjoy the peace that only relationship with Him can bring. The Scriptures declare this clearly:

> For if, when we were enemies, we were reconciled to God by the death of his Son, much more, being reconciled, we shall be saved by his life. And not only so, but we also joy in God through our LORD Jesus Christ, by whom we have now received the atonement.
> —ROMANS 5:10–11

Peace with God and true purpose and meaning for life are available to anyone who chooses to accept Jesus and learns to obey His commands. Only those who first experience the spiritual reality of this new birth have the hope of attaining true heart satisfaction. All of Jesus' promises for love, joy, and peace are for those who receive Him as their Savior. He said that He came to give abundant life and to satisfy the thirst of our souls in such a way that we would never thirst again (John 4:10,14).

THE CHRISTIAN'S DILEMMA

Having said that we must qualify the promise of abundant life as being available for those who accept Christ as their Savior, we must qualify it even further. The Scriptures are clear that Jesus' promise is for those Christians who continue to cultivate their relationship with Him according to His revealed will in the Word of God. To enjoy intimate human relationship requires that two people walk in fellowship on a continual basis, learning to know and care for each other more deeply each day. The same is true in our relationship with God.

It would be ridiculous, for example, to think that marriage could be enjoyed if, after meeting the bride-to-be on one occasion, the bridegroom never saw her again. Only as he develops a relationship with her, winning her heart to his and setting goals for their lives together, can he ever expect to enjoy the commitment and communion of his wedding night. Yet, as Christians, we sometimes act as if we should enjoy the benefits of a marriage relationship with God when we are barely on speaking terms with Him, and that only occasionally.

PEACE THROUGH RECONCILIATION

Webster defines the verb *reconcile* as "to restore to friendship or harmony; to settle and resolve differences." Being reconciled to God begins with the new birth experience. But it does not end there. In order to enjoy peace with God we must be reconciled to Him in every area of our lives throughout our lives. To enjoy such a state of reconciliation requires a process of learning to yield to His will for our lives.

The Scriptures also teach us to "let the peace of God rule in your hearts" (Col. 3:15). Another version states emphatically that the peace of God should "(act as umpire continually) in your hearts [deciding and settling with finality all questions that arise in your minds]" (AMP).

As a child, I learned from my dad and my brothers that you

never question an umpire—his word is final. So when I read this verse as a teenager, I understood that the peace of God was to be the deciding factor in every decision I made, every word I spoke, every relationship and activity in which I was involved. That truth has become such a reality to me that when my peace is disturbed, I know instinctively that I must change my course, my attitude, or my decision in a certain situation. The umpire—the peace of God—has disagreed with my course of action, and I am not willing to live with the misery I experience when I am not reconciled to Him.

We learn to let peace rule in our hearts by submitting our lives to God in everyday situations. Jesus is called the Prince of Peace (Isa. 9:6). And He shows us the path to take many times simply by letting us experience His "peace that passes understanding," even when the path seems contrary to logic. At other times, we may feel a lack of inner peace about a choice or a relationship that we are pursuing, though outwardly it seems right to us. We will never be sorry if we learn to listen to our Guide, letting the Prince of Peace reign as umpire in all our decisions.

HUMAN PURSUITS

The basic pursuits of every human heart are essentially the same, united as we are by our desperate humanness. For example, we may do different things to be accepted by others, but the basic human need we are seeking to fulfill is the need for approval. We seek employment that will meet our need for financial security. And it is natural to want to fall in love in our youth with Mr. or Miss Wonderful who will always be there for us. However, if we insist on basing our search for contentment on the approval of those around us, on financial security, on romance, or other basic human pursuits, we will never enjoy the peace of reconciliation and true heart satisfaction that comes from submitting our choices, our desires, and our pursuits to God's will.

The demands we place on people and circumstances to satisfy our desires are first of all not fair. And second, they cannot bring predictably desirable results. They are not fair because God did not intend for us to look to people or circumstances to meet our deepest needs for fulfillment. When we do, we are sure to choose relationships and employment situations motivated by what we can get out of them, rather than by what we can give to them. When they do not give us what we are looking for, we feel victimized. And other people's responses to us are unpredictable because they are living life from their own perspectives, trying to get their needs met, just as we are.

When my world of relationships, place of ministry, and job security fell apart, my peace was shattered, and I knew I had to find God in my painful situation. I began to read books written by Christian psychologists that are written to help us "put our lives back together." They were helpful to me to the extent that they directed me to God and to His Word, sometimes interpreting the Scriptures that applied to my present distress, showing me how to be reconciled to God. Beyond that, however, I did not find lasting relief from these self-help books.

One evening as I was reading one of these books, looking for answers to my emotional pain, the Lord spoke these words to me: "I want you to take your self-esteem from Me." I was so startled at the force with which these words came to my heart and the import of their meaning, that I almost lost my breath.

Putting the book down, I pondered His statement before asking, "Lord, is that possible? Can You communicate to me so personally that I would know Your approval and feel accepted and esteemed apart from human affirmation? Can I hear You so clearly that my wounded spirit would be healed and the rejection I am feeling dispelled?"

A few weeks later, I received a prophetic word through the laying on of hands of the presbytery that publicly affirmed the blessing of God on my life and denounced accusations that had been spoken against me by some who were present in the assembly. The prophetic exhortation was filled with the favor and blessing of God and promise of my future fruitfulness in the kingdom, which was the desire of my heart. In those few moments of public, divine affirmation, my heart was healed, the emotional pain disappeared, and I rejoiced in renewed hope for the future. I had never experienced the peace of God before as profoundly as I did in those moments.

That was several years ago, and to this day I am walking in the wonderful deliverance that prophetic word brought to me. The Lord had proved to me that He could indeed affirm me in such a way that my psychological bondages would be utterly destroyed. In seeking His approval and submitting my "choices" to Him, I found a place of reconciliation and peace with God that I had not known before. And I walk in greater liberty than I ever experienced from seeking the approval of men to feel valuable as a person.

Of course, the prophetic anointing that brings the peace of God to our hearts resides on the Scriptures themselves. As we read them diligently, the Holy Spirit will breathe His life into our spirits, and we will be set free from our emotional and psychological bondages. Jesus said, "And ye shall know the truth, and the truth shall make you free" (John 8:32). The truth of the Word can destroy every yoke of bondage upon our minds and hearts that robs us of peace as we allow Him to wash us with the water of the Word (Eph. 5:26).

Choosing to obey the Word of God—not just hear it—is the key to our deliverance (James 1:22). Psychological principles that do not violate or substitute for the truths of the Scriptures can help us to identify wrong thinking patterns. But knowing what is wrong with us is not the same as fixing it. And natural mental exercises are not enough to overcome supernatural bondages.

There is nothing as powerful and liberating as the Word of God, written or spoken prophetically, to change our hearts and set us free from our bondages. The Scriptures show us when we need to repent, forgive, and turn from certain ways of thinking, doing, or relating. For example, a simple revelation of the truth, "He hath made us accepted in the beloved," (Eph. 1:6) can break the power of rejection over our lives without having to determine through extensive psychological therapy why we feel rejected, who rejected us, and when it all happened.

The apostle James exhorted us to "receive with meekness the engrafted word, which is able to save your souls" (James 1:21). Another version says it "contains the power to save your souls" (AMP). Our souls—our intellect, will, and emotions—desperately need to be saved. Even after our spirits are born again, we need to allow the Word to live in us to redeem—buy back—our souls and reconcile us to the will of God.

As we find deliverance through the Word and seek to be completely reconciled to God in every area of our lives, we take the unfair burden off our marriage, our children, our employer, our friends, our pastor, and even our circumstances to meet our emotional needs and "make us happy." When we are living in relationship with God, knowing His peace, feeling loved and accepted, we will be able to bring to our relationships those same qualities.

As we give love and acceptance freely in all our relationships and life situations, we will discover the positive, constructive effect of Jesus' words: "It is more blessed to give than to receive" (Acts 20:35). Without that love of God working divine reconciliation in our emotions and psyches, we are stuck in the universal dilemma of discontent that has destroyed mankind since the beginning of time.

For some of the same reasons we have mentioned earlier—fear of addressing our deep inner discontent, lack of relationships in which to discuss it, and yielding to worldly mindsets and media deceptions that promise contentment—even many born-again Christians who are pursuing a relationship with God have not experienced true heart satisfaction. Sadly, the church has sometimes inadvertently given believers at least one more reason for not discovering the heart satisfaction available to the children of God.

The church has often been guilty of duplicating the world's "ideas" of finding satisfaction through the humanistic approach of self-realization. "Ministry" positions, prestige, and power as they are defined within a particular church structure are pursued by sincere Christians who are trying to satisfy their psyche's need for approval, acceptance, and self-esteem by serving in the church. These believers inevitably experience the same disappointing results from seeking satisfaction from false sources as the non-Christians experience in their temporal pursuits.

From the hierarchy of episcopal forms of church government to the five-fold ministry gifts of charismatic church structure, all who seek, however sincerely, to find fulfillment through church-defined success are doomed to disappointment, at best, and deception, at worst. Heart satisfaction that is only found in relationship with God can never be replaced by anything even as good as serving the church.

We are not endorsing relationship with God without service to the church and to the community. To the contrary, true reconciliation to God will bring us into effective service for the glory of God. Yet it is sadly true that many people who are actively serving the church have lost sight of their priority of relationship with God. The familiar saying is true: "He became so busy with the work of the Lord that he lost sight of the Lord of the work." Unfortunately, that reality manifests in many sincere Christians' lives. They have not yet reconciled their personal ambitions to the will of God for their lives.

"CHRISTIAN" HUMANISM

I was born again when I was eight years old, raised in a Pentecostal minister's home, and have served God since I was a child. Having lived more than thirty years as an adult, I have found myself submitting, sometimes reluctantly, to the "legitimate" psychological drives that are peculiar to our "adult species." I have spent years seeking satisfaction through the pursuit of Christian relationships and service to the church. While I do not regret any of my service to the Lord, I have become keenly aware that my motivation has at times been contaminated with a mixture of desire to please the Lord along with other human needs for approval, acceptance, and (shall I say it?) self-realization.

In Search of *Peace*

The disappointments we suffer in not having our ego needs met can serve us well if they drive us to seek God in our pain. As the Holy Spirit reveals to us the mixture in our motives and cleanses our hearts from the humanistic desire of self-realization, He will give us the desire to truly have a servant's heart as Jesus demonstrated to us. Becoming reconciled to God in our inner motivation brings peace beyond description as we desire to please Him alone. Ironically, it is much easier to please God than it is to please man. When we live to serve God alone, we can enjoy His favor on our lives through our obedience to Him even when people are criticizing the job we are doing.

The picture of Jesus' seven-fold humbling of Himself to become a man and a servant of men has always been exquisitely beautiful to me. (See Philippians 2.) But how difficult it is to our minds and hearts when the Holy Spirit leads us down a similar path to servanthood in order that our pride can be reconciled to the humility of God. The pride of our hearts despises that way, desiring instead to ascend to personal greatness through self-realization.

Not only our wrong motivation and our pride, but even the drives that are basic to all mature (I use the term loosely) human beings must be reconciled to God in order for peace to rule in our hearts. For example, the natural appetite for food is necessary for the maintenance of life, but if we let it rule our lives, we will become victims of gluttony. And gluttony is not only the sin of the obese. Many born-again Christians today suffer from eating disorders and food addictions because they have not yet been reconciled to God in this area of natural appetite.

A certain amount of rest and sleep is required daily for our bodies and minds to function normally. But if we allow ourselves to become slothful, indulging ourselves in sleeping away the day, we will come to poverty, according to the Scriptures (Prov. 20:13). Every legitimate human drive must become rightly related to the divine priority of seeking the kingdom of God first if we are to enjoy the peace that comes from divine reconciliation. Otherwise we will become victims of one or more of our natural appetites that will gain dominion in our lives.

THE POWER OF CHOICE

So overwhelming has been the influence of secular humanism in our educational system that many Christians are subconsciously nurturing the philosophy of developing the kingdom of "self" in their lives and in the lives of their children rather than the virtues of Christian character. For them, the child's self-realization of his or her desires and choices must be considered above all else. This is an ungodly priority that masquerades as caring, godly parenting. In order to become mature Christians enjoying fulfillment in God, our desires and choices must be reconciled to the will of God.

By placing too high a priority on our children's psychological welfare we may inadvertently burden them with too many choices at too early an age. And if we do not take into account the basic sinful nature of a child who needs to be born again, we can be guilty of strengthening their natural psyches to embrace a false sense of self-sufficiency through exercising their power of choice. We need to teach them that our first priority is to choose to yield our hearts to God and be reconciled to Him in every area of our lives.

One hot summer evening, a friend who was visiting from another country and I decided to go out to get some ice cream. We went to the ice cream shop where there were twenty-nine different flavors from which to choose. My friend became quite distraught. He looked at every flavor and tasted several but could not decide what to buy. Then he looked again and tasted others. Finally, in exasperation, he exclaimed, "The problem with Americans is you have too many choices!"

Though our choice of a flavor of ice cream is not a vital spiritual issue, I believe his observation touches a nerve of our society's ills at large. We become so absorbed with the variety of choices—cereal, houses, cars, clothes, and even marriage partners and churches—that we expect to find fulfillment through making the "right choice." And if it doesn't work, we can always choose again. Such thinking makes the power of choice an idol that replaces the desire and will of God for us. And idols will never deliver the satisfaction that our hearts so desperately crave.

A. W. Tozer has this to say about our choices:

> Our choices reveal what kind of persons we are, but there is another side to the coin. We may by our choices also determine what kind of persons we will become. We humans are not only in a state of being, we are in a state of becoming; we are on a slow spiral moving gradually up or down. Here we move not singly but in companies, and we are drawn to these companies by the attraction of similarity. I think it might be well for us to check our spiritual condition occasionally by the simple test of compatibility. When we are free to go, where do we go? In what company do we feel most at home? Where do our thoughts turn when they are free to turn where they will? The answer to these questions may tell us more about ourselves than we can comfortably accept.[4]

Every situation we encounter offers the opportunity of choosing to respond according to the character of Christ who dwells within us or according to our self-life that has a propensity toward sin. We decide continually who we will become as we choose to respond to the people and circumstances in our lives.

CHOOSING TO BE RECONCILED TO GOD

After the apostle Paul had pursued great learning and attained great recognition in the religious society of the day, having been born with the right pedigree of Jewish distinction, he declared that he counted all those things as loss that he might know Christ. He declared that he suffered the loss of all things in order to win Christ (Phil. 3:8). Has the gospel

53

changed for us? Was this just the passion of an apostle who had a special mission for God?

We may not place much value on the loss of the particular things Paul lists. But if we substitute the things he valued for the things we value so highly, perhaps we can relate to his revelation of the true worth of all that the world (and religion) can offer us. It is not to be compared to the priceless treasure of knowing Christ intimately. Paul said that what he counted as "gain" was "dung" compared to the value of his relationship with Christ. We must be able to say the same about the things we value if we are to know Christ as He did.

Perhaps the writers of the past—Oswald Chambers, A.W. Tozer, F. B. Meier and others—were too austere in their outlook on life. Oswald Chambers, for example, defined selfishness as "that which gives me pleasure without considering Jesus Christ's interests."[5] He defined self-realization in this way:

> God is the only One who has the right to myself, and when I love Him with all my heart and soul and mind and strength, self in its essence is realized.[6]

He understood that loving God with all our heart, soul, mind, and strength brings us into perfect reconciliation with the will of God. Chambers also describes true heart fulfillment:

> If anyone understood me, he would be my god. The only Being Who understands me is the Being Who made me and Who redeems me, and He will never expound me to myself; He will only bring me to the place of reality, viz., into contact with Himself, and the heart is at leisure from itself for ever afterwards."[7]

What a beautiful word picture Oswald Chambers paints of a "heart at leisure from itself." This is not the result of an austere religious philosophy but of an intimate relationship with God. Such peace is not reserved for us in heaven, but can be experienced now by the one who is willing to be reconciled to God alone.

Does this sound like radical theology to our ears? If so, perhaps it is because we have become victims of the philosophy of "Christian humanism" that has the same goal as secular humanism—that of self-realization, becoming our own gods through self-determination. We would, of course, alter our lifestyles to fit our acceptable Christian traditions. But if we do not seek complete reconciliation with God, we remain in charge, never coming to the reality of surrender to God described by Chambers, which brings the heart to ultimate "leisure."

As born-again Christians who are filled with many temporal pursuits, we have to be honest enough to admit that we suffer personal discontent with life in order to turn our hearts to the source of true contentment. As we choose to seek God above all else, asking Him to shine His light on our hearts, He will show us the path of life. The Scriptures teach us that if we will acknowledge Him in all our ways He will direct our paths (Prov. 3:6).

PERSONAL RESPONSIBILITY

Our purpose for discussing the futility of seeking heart satisfaction in the places we have mentioned (which are not exhaustive) is not to arouse a sense of hopelessness about ever finding contentment. On the contrary, we must first believe, as we have stated, that personal heart satisfaction is not only possible, but is the very heart and purpose of God for humanity. Otherwise, we would not dare to address this universal problem of discontent.

Unless we are willing to admit, however, that having sought satisfaction in some wrong places, we continue to suffer the pain of personal discontent, we can never hope to break its deception over our minds and discover the secrets of true contentment. Neither can we expect to find true satisfaction if we blame circumstances or relationships for our lack of contentment. We must accept personal responsibility for searching in the wrong places for heart satisfaction and repent for our deception. Even discovering the secrets for finding the

The Satisfied Heart

heart satisfaction that God has promised cannot help us if we are not willing to take personal responsibility for our discontent and renounce the false sources of contentment we have embraced. That is part of the price tag attached to finding true life satisfaction.

In the case of those who have lived in denial and refused to face their inner discontent, they must dare to be honest with themselves and admit that life is not as satisfying as they pretend—that they are indeed victims of the howling wolf of discontent. Then they can begin to look for heart satisfaction in the right place—through cultivating relationship with God.

Though it will cost us to seek for true contentment, the rewards for finding heart satisfaction cannot be measured in this life alone. They will continue to multiply to us throughout eternity. Isaiah declared: "For since the beginning of the world men have not heard, nor perceived by the ear, neither hath the eye seen, O God, beside thee, what he hath prepared for him that waiteth for him" (Isa. 64:4). If we feel an unwillingness to pay the price to find true satisfaction, it may help us to realize that living in a false sense of contentment also has its price—one which is often collected in a moment of personal tragedy, bankrupting our entire futures.

While God does not offer us immediate gratification (as most media ads do), He does promise continuing and increasing heart satisfaction as we learn to walk in the principles He has given us to be reconciled to Him, not only for eternity, but for this life as well. We have much to gain and nothing—except our painful deceptions—to lose by yielding to God's way in our pursuit of satisfaction.

No matter how inordinately bound we may be to our apparent source of contentment—whether as carnal as food, as spiritual as ministry, or as necessary as intimate relationships—we can be delivered to enjoy true heart satisfaction. Truth has the power to break the deceptions in our minds that rob us of the contentment God has promised. In our pursuit of peace with God and others, when we know what God's perspective is and learn to embrace it, we will begin to rejoice in His definition of "abundant life" for us.

The "exchanged life"—His quality of life for our self-life—becomes a reality to us. The New Testament commands us: "Be ye transformed by the renewing of your mind" (Rom. 12:2). We exchange our faulty way of reasoning for His life-giving thoughts; our wrong attachment to people and things, places and positions for His emotional freedom; our frenzied service for His restful yoke.

What do we have to lose as we consider God's provision for us in the vital pursuits of life? Only our bondage to wrong thinking patterns, pursuits, and relationships that will loose their hold on our minds and emotions as we experience wholeness through intimate relationship with God.

CHAPTER 4

In Search of

Intimacy

Enjoying Divine Relationship

He is intimate with the upright.
—Proverbs 3:32, NAS

As a teenager, I had a deep hunger to know God. In my pursuit of God, I set aside time every day to read His Word and pray, waiting on Him sometimes entire evenings alone in my room. One evening as I was praying alone in my bedroom, suddenly I felt as if someone turned on a movie projector in my mind. I began to see a vision unfold before me. I was watching it, yet at the same time I felt as though I were the one acting it out. At first all I saw was darkness. It was dark in my bedroom, but this darkness I was "seeing" was different; it was frightening. I had never been afraid of the dark. Yet this darkness was menacing in its blackness. As I watched, I saw a man groping about in the frightening darkness. He seemed lost and alone and very sad.

As I continued to watch, in the distance I saw a softly glowing light. As I focused my attention on that light, I saw what appeared to be a single light bulb, without a globe or any attractiveness, hanging over a doorway. The lone traveler,

59

The Satisfied Heart

groping along in the murky darkness, saw the light when I did and started toward it. I sensed his relief as he approached the doorway over which the single light bulb shone. As he stood in that light, I could see him more clearly. It was then I noticed that he had a huge pack on his back and that he was bent over under the weight of it.

As he stood in that light, I felt his relief as though it were mine. Then he entered the doorway over which the light hung. Though there were no printed signs, as I watched I knew that the man had just entered the door of salvation. As he stood beyond in a comfortable room, his eyes became accustomed to the light. He seemed peaceful now. The torment of that spiritual darkness had been left behind.

After a while, the man looked straight ahead of him and saw another doorway similar to the first that he had just entered. Without hesitation he entered it. The room in which he found himself was bigger and the light was more intense. And I understood that he had experienced the baptism of the Holy Spirit. He enjoyed more liberty here and basked in the wonderful warmth of his surroundings.

As his eyes became accustomed to the greater light here, I saw him look straight ahead once again to another doorway. He was obviously feeling safe and happy on this lighted pathway he had found, and as soon as he saw the doorway, he attempted to enter it as he had done before.

This time, however, he did not fit through the doorway. Surprised, he stopped to see what was impeding his progress. When he looked over his shoulder, he became aware of the huge pack on his back. I instinctively knew that pack represented "self." Without thinking about it, the man quickly threw off several peripheral items from the pack so that it was smaller, and he entered through that doorway into the next room. To his delight, he found this room to be larger still and the light even brighter than where he had come from. Added to that joy was the relief from throwing off some of the weight of that huge pack he carried on his back.

As I watched, this process continued. When the man

became accustomed to the light in one room, he saw the next doorway in front of him (there were no doors on the entrances), and he would attempt to go through it. Always there was more of the pack to lay aside, for each doorway was smaller than the previous one. I don't know how many doorways he entered. But each doorway he went through brought him into greater liberty where the light was more intense. His burden of self—that huge pack on his back— was smaller and easier to carry after laying aside more of it at each smaller doorway.

Finally, the man came to what I instinctively knew was the last doorway. There was no pack on the man's back now. But the doorway was so small that he had to get on his knees to crawl through it. Without hesitation, he started to go through it, but though he was crouched low on hands and knees, he did not fit. Backing up, he looked over his shoulder and reached up to feel a tiny package still resting between his shoulders. Small as it was, that package would not allow him to get through this last doorway.

I saw the man take that little package into his hands and look at it tenderly. In that moment I understood that it was the dearest thing to his heart. I felt his anguish as he faced a terrible decision. He would have to lay aside the dearest desire of his heart in order to take the next step in his walk with God. For the first time, he looked back through every doorway he had entered, until his eyes rested on the tiny light over the first doorway. Then he looked past it into the outer darkness from which he had come.

It was a frightening moment. As he knelt there I felt as if I were the one in that terrible moment of decision. I watched him turn back toward the doorway, slowly, painfully, still looking at the precious package that he held in his hands. Trembling, he laid it down beside that doorway and disappeared from my view as he entered that last place. As he crawled through that doorway, I felt personally, the wonderful presence of God. Inexplicably, I understood that he had disappeared into the very heart of God.

The Satisfied Heart

I felt such rest, peace, contentment, fulfillment kneeling there in my bedroom in those moments of revelation as I had never known in my walk with God. Immediately I concluded that the man had gone to heaven, which is what fit my theology at the time. *This must be what heaven feels like*, I thought. It was several years later that I began to realize that God wants us to know that intimacy of union with Him through our complete surrender to Him while we live on this earth.

It was this intimate relationship that Jesus enjoyed with His Father as He walked in perfect harmony with the will of God in every moment of His earthly life. And it was to this wonderful quality of life that Jesus referred when He prayed for us: "And this is life eternal, that they might know thee the only true God, and Jesus Christ, whom thou hast sent" (John 17:3). It was Jesus' delight to do the will of the Father, and He knows that as we learn to know God, we will experience the same delight of eternal life that He did. Jesus showed us how to walk in obedience so that we can enjoy the satisfaction of intimate relationship with the Father and enjoy eternal life here on earth.

INTIMACY DEFINED

Hollywood has exploited the legitimate human cry for intimacy, creating a billion-dollar enterprise of so-called romantic movies that have redefined morality for an entire culture. Their focus on sexual intimacy as the crown jewel of human experience has caused many to despair in the face of real-life relationships where the fantasies of the cinema are not realized. Some disillusioned souls are seduced from one empty relationship to another, much as a desert wanderer who follows the mirage images of cool pools of water across the hot, burning sand dunes, tormented by his unquenchable thirst, searching for the ecstasy that has eluded him.

What is intimacy? It seems reasonable to ask the question, given the universality of our insatiable need to experience intimacy, as well as the apparent unhappiness that millions suffer, searching for it in all the wrong places. If we accept

Hollywood's definition of intimacy, we must embrace the idea
that we can fulfill our need for intimacy through sexual experience with any partner who offers satisfying, though often
short-lived and not necessarily romantic, intercourse.

This blatant disregard for biblical morality has seduced millions into thinking they have a right to choose their sexual
partners without regard to the fidelity of the marriage covenant
taught in the Scriptures. The results of embracing this hedo-
nistic philosophy are seen today in the "live-in" lifestyle that is
replacing a society of solid homes and families, in the epidemic
of sexually transmitted diseases, and in the soaring divorce rate.
And for all this, we have failed to find the satisfaction of intimacy in relationship for which we are desperately searching.

Even the church, though teaching biblical standards of
morality, home, and family, has been deeply influenced by the
romantic heresy of Hollywood. Many Christian young people
expect to experience the epitome of romance in their search
for their mates, placing more value on physical appearance
and attraction than on the will and purpose of God for their
lives. This worldly perspective has given rise to promiscuity
among church youth who, sometimes unwittingly, find themselves trying out their prospective mates according to this
worldly philosophy. Premarital sex is touted as the norm rather
than the exception among our youth today.

It may help to give objectivity to our perspective on
romantic love to simply consider that there are entire cultures
that have not bought into the deception that romance determines happiness. In some cultures dating is not even practiced
and romance is not a requirement for marriage. In India, for
example, marriages are still arranged by the parents and
entered into without the perilous practice of dating. While we
may feel this is an archaic arrangement and that our culture
has been liberated from such unthinkable restraints, we would
do well to compare the divorce rates and results of promiscuity of our nation to those of India. Divorce as well as
diseases caused by promiscuity are uncommon there. Without
the fantasy expectations of romance to haunt them, the youth

of this culture choose to love the person chosen for them and safely enter into marriage, accepting personal responsibility for their own marriage happiness.

If Hollywood's pervasive definition of intimacy has so corrupted our entire society, making its deadly influence felt even in the church, where do we go to find an antidote? Truth is always the antidote for deception. Hollywood's deception lies not only in the breaking of biblical codes of morality, but also in its narrow, faulty definition of intimacy. It will help us to replace Hollywood's definition of intimacy with a more accurate one. Webster defines the word *intimate* as "intrinsic, essential, belonging to or characterizing one's deepest nature. It suggests informal warmth or privacy, deep friendship developed through long association, and of a very personal and private nature."

Sexual intimacy, while intended by God to be a wonderful state of ecstasy between husband and wife, is not the ultimate satisfaction for the universal human cry for intimacy. To suggest that it is violates the innate heart cry for intimacy of every man, woman, and child. It condemns the single person to a life of dissatisfaction while it frustrates married people, causing disillusionment with marriage. Many single people who have accepted Hollywood's version of romance as the source of fulfillment live in emotional anguish, feeling they will never know happiness without experiencing sexual intimacy. And married people who expect to reach an unattainable state of ultimate satisfaction through sexual intimacy suffer from disappointment when it fails to satisfy the deeper cry of their hearts for true intimacy.

Many helpful books have been written to teach Christians how to deepen their relationships with their spouses and overcome this wrong concept of intimacy that our culture has absorbed. True intimacy, even on a human level, involves caring and meaningful communication, thoughtfulness, sacrificial giving, respect, and trust. These are elements in a marriage relationship that give meaning and significance to physical intimacy. When these qualities are lacking in marriage, many married people look to friendships outside of their marriage, either with the same sex or with the opposite sex, to fulfill emotional needs that are not met by their spouses.

Though the need for friendship relationships is legitimate and can complement a healthy marriage, we cannot expect spouse or friends to satisfy our heart cry for intimacy. If we do, the emotional demands we place on these relationships will become unbearable, resulting in neurotic dependencies and other unhealthy relationships. Our cry for intimacy can be truly satisfied only in our relationship with God. Until we embrace this reality, we cannot expect to find satisfaction, no matter how wonderful our human relationships may be.

If we accept the biblical argument that man was made for God, then we must look beyond the need for sexual intimacy to find the essence of intimacy that will satisfy the human heart. Indeed, we must look beyond human relationship of any kind if we expect to discover and enjoy intimacy that is "intrinsic" and "essential" to human happiness and fulfillment.

Even Webster's definition of intimacy defies Hollywood's idea of casual romantic relationships by stating that intimacy is experienced through deep friendship developed by long association. It suggests that time of association is required in order to develop a truly intimate relationship. And Webster's definition does not make sexual involvement necessary for intimacy to be realized in a relationship. So much for "one night stands." By definition we at least have to accept that there is more involved in enjoying true intimacy than attempting to satisfy our sexuality. To discover what *is* involved in experiencing true intimacy that will satisfy the intrinsic longing of our deepest nature, we must turn to the Word of God for definition.

INTIMACY WITH GOD

> For the crooked man is an abomination to the LORD;
> but He is intimate with the upright.
>
> —PROVERBS 3:32, NAS

The Satisfied Heart

The word in the Hebrew translated intimate in Proverbs 3:32 means "to sit down together, to counsel and instruct, to establish, to settle, and to share inward secrets." The Bible declares that God is intimate with the righteous. That is, He sits down with them to counsel, instruct, and share secrets with them. To sit down with God in an intimate setting, sharing His heart and mind, seems almost a greater fantasy than the ecstasy Hollywood promises in its narrow definition of intimacy.

I have tried to imagine what it would have been like to be Eve before she sinned, walking in the garden in the cool of the day with God, enjoying the comfort of His presence, listening to His voice. Is it possible to know God in such a way that I can feel His nearness and commune with Him intelligibly? Can I really satisfy my seemingly insatiable cry for intimacy by relating to a God I cannot see? Or touch?

Emphatically, the answer is *yes*! More emphatically, there is no other relationship that can satisfy this intrinsic, primary need so entwined with the very essence of our person. God alone can establish us and give us instruction that brings wholeness and purpose to our lives, revealing our eternal destiny, and fulfilling heart desires that He has given. The Scriptures promise this kind of satisfying relationship with God to those who will seek Him with their whole hearts. They teach that God's desire for relationship with mankind is the passion of all He has ever done. From the initial creation of man to sending His Son to die for our redemption, the entire plan of the universe revolves around God's desire for a family, for sons and daughters to whom He can demonstrate His great love.

The Scriptures declare that God is love. God Himself defines love in its essence. He reveals to us the true nature of love. It follows then, that without knowing God, we will never truly experience love as God created us to know it. Oswald Chambers describes God's love in its awesome power:

> Love in the Bible is ONE; it is unique, and the human element is but one aspect of it. It is a love so mighty, so absorbing, so intense that all the mind is emancipated

and entranced by God; all the heart is transfigured by the same devotion; all the soul in its living, working, waking, sleeping moments is indwelt and surrounded and enwheeled in the rest of this love.[8]

We have stated that because man was made for God, he can only find fulfillment in the restoration of his relationship with God. Our hunger for intimacy is ordained to draw us to the heart of God where we can find true fulfillment. Only in that intimate relationship—our heart reunited to the heart of the Father—can the intrinsic, deepest need of our nature be realized. Again, Oswald Chambers comments on the nature of our love for the Lord:

Love for the LORD is not an ethereal, intellectual, dream-like thing; it is the most intense, the most vital, the most passionate love of which the human heart is capable.[9]

Intense, vital, passionate—these qualities should characterize our love for God. Because of the deception of sin, we have focused our emotional energies on human relationships, looking in all the wrong places to find the deep satisfaction for intimate love that we crave. Only the truth can set us free to seek true intimacy with God, where it can be found. To the degree that we find satisfaction in our relationship with God, our human relationships will be healthy and fulfilling, and we will have true love to give family and friends. Writing about human love, Oswald Chambers clarifies:

The Bible makes no distinction between Divine love and human love, it speaks only of "love." Jesus says I must love God with all my heart and soul and mind and strength, then my love for my fellow men will be relative to that centre . . .The love which has God as its centre makes no demands. The reward of love is the capacity to pour out more love all the time, hoping for nothing again. That is the essential nature of perfect love.[10]

The Satisfied Heart

This intimate relationship with God is the answer to the despair of the single person who has given his life to God and yet struggles against the prototypes of a society that condemns singles to dissatisfaction or worse. It is the answer to the married person who is disillusioned in his marriage relationship, having placed expectations on his spouse that are not humanly possible to fulfill. Abandoning ourselves to love God with all our being will result in His pouring Himself, His nature, His love, into our hearts until we are truly satisfied and are able to give love to others that will satisfy them as well.

Accepting the fact that human relationships, no matter how noble and self-sacrificing and godly, were not meant to ultimately fulfill our cry for intimacy, is one of the most liberating truths of the gospel. Only by accepting this truth can we begin to enter into our search for fulfillment that will take us to the source of that fulfillment—the heart of God.

As we focus our minds and hearts toward God, expecting Him to become to us the satisfaction and fulfillment we so desperately need, we begin a journey that leads us to indescribable joy and peace and, yes, intimacy, that no human being could ever give to us. People around us may look with pity at our outward status, evaluating our potential for happiness by our possessions or human relationships. But if we are daily consumed with our journey into true fulfillment, giving ourselves to the Word, to prayer, and to obedience to the revelation of God's will, we will become so satisfied in Him that it will be our turn to pity those around us who have not found God to be the source of their fulfillment.

It is no wonder that evolutionists, atheists, humanists, and existentialists (all varieties of the same theme) who look to themselves as gods, determining their own course, are doomed to disillusionment, despair, and ultimate destruction. A society that has abandoned its intrinsic needs of personhood to lesser gods of intellectualism, materialism, and individualism, offers no hope to individuals longing for heart satisfaction.

And to the degree that the church allows itself to be influenced by its culture, letting godless philosophies erode the central focus of the Word of God and its power to transform our lives, Christians will experience the same destructions as our unchurched counterparts. We dare not look for fulfillment of our deepest desires for intimacy anywhere other than in our relationship with God. No matter how "Christian" our pursuits may appear, or how godly our relationships, they are certain to disappoint us if we are not nurturing our secret, inward relationship with God.

The psalmist David lived a life of intimacy with God even as a boy shepherd in the hills of Judea. The love and admiration he expressed toward God in the many psalms he wrote were not just words or abstract ideas but heart-felt experiences of revelation of the heart of God. He declared, "The secret of the LORD is with them that fear him; and he will shew them his covenant"(Ps.25:14). The word *secret* means "counsel" or "intimacy." Those who reverence God and seek to know Him will not be disappointed. Their hearts will be satisfied with the intimate response of their Creator, who will show them the love and security of His covenant.

Covenant is a concept that has been terribly maligned in our culture. While we do not intend to discuss it fully here, it may be helpful to note that covenant is the unbreakable agreement of relationship that brings the security to our hearts and lives that we so desperately need. Enjoying covenant relationship with the essence of love, God Himself, brings the greatest rest to the human psyche and emotions that can be known. There is no fear of betrayal here, nor of any harm, for love cannot allow harm to come to its beloved. Complete openness—an essential element in intimacy—is not only possible but desirable in such a trustworthy relationship.

One New Testament writer declared: "All things are open and laid bare to the eyes of Him with whom we have to do" (Heb. 4:13, NAS). To some that is a fearful text, especially if they are not cultivating an intimate relationship with God. But true intimacy cannot be realized without true knowing—one of another—that comes from complete openness. It is a rare and noble relationship between friends or spouses that can come near to this requisite of intimacy. The deepest secrets of the heart can only be shared in an atmosphere of complete trust without fear of unseemly disclosure.

Jesus declared that He did nothing but what He saw the Father doing (John 5:19). He was completely dependent on His relationship with His Father for every word He spoke and every action He did. His words and actions were completely dependent on His intimate relationship with His Father. This openness to His Father's will resulted in the heart satisfaction that He expressed when He said, "My food is to do the will of Him who sent me, and to accomplish His work" (John 4:34).

I have read of the many times that Jesus spent the night in prayer with His Father, and I have admired Him for such a sacrifice of sleep and time, and for enduring such aloneness. How mistaken I found my judgment to be when I began to enjoy personal intimacy of relationship in prayer with God.

The wonder of hearing God's secret counsel and finding security, rest, direction, and fulfillment for life through such counsel cannot be considered sacrifice. For me, these seasons of prayer have been the most blessed times of my life. One phrase whispered to my heart in our quiet times of intimacy thrills and sustains me for weeks in the joy of His expressed love. His presence sets me free from bondages to sin and self and strengthens me for the tasks He has given me to do.

Jesus said, "I do not seek My own will but the will of the Father who sent me" (John 5:30, NKJV). Later He told His disciples, "As the Father has sent Me, I also send you" (John 20:21, NKJV). He expects us to enjoy the same intimacy that He knew with His Father when He walked this earth. How low have been our expectations of relationship with God! Even devout Christians think it unusual to "hear" the voice of God personally or to sense His nearness and His comfort. Many have not understood that it is God's plan for our fulfillment to enjoy intimate relationship with Him.

It is not difficult to experience intimacy with God. Cultivating regular times of prayer and reading the Word, learning to "acknowledge Him in all of our ways" during our day — these are simple exercises of our hearts and minds that create an atmosphere for divine intimacy. Surrender to His revealed will deepens that relationship and prepares us for greater revelation of our personal destiny.

Yet even many Christians who attempt to establish a personal devotional life admit that they do not enjoy the depths of intimacy we are describing. Why? I believe it is simply because they have not *expected* God to meet with them in that meaningful way. And they have not believed that He alone can satisfy the deepest longings of their heart.

When we are convinced that God gave us our intrinsic desires for intimacy and that He longs to fulfill those desires, we will begin to search the Word and seek times of prayer alone, to cultivate an intimate relationship with God. The Scriptures plainly declare that if you "draw near to God . . . He will draw near to you" (James 4:8, NKJV).

The good news of the gospel is that our deepest human needs for intimacy can be fulfilled regardless of our marital status, our economic status, our culture's values, or our present relationships. Accepting that good news will bring us the freedom to pursue our deepest personal fulfillment through seeking intimate relationship with God. I do not believe anyone who takes that challenge will ever be disappointed.

Not only the Bible but history itself records the passion of saints and martyrs who despised everything this world had offered when compared to the fulfillment and satisfaction they had found in relationship with God. Nicolas of Cusa, an early saint, wrote:

> When the habit of inwardly gazing Godward becomes fixed within us we shall be ushered onto a new level of spiritual life more in keeping with the promises of God and the mood of the New Testament The Triune God will be our dwelling place even while our feet walk the low road of simple duty here among men. We will have found life's *summum bonum* indeed. There is the source of all delights that can be desired; not only can nought better be thought out by men and angels, but

nought better can exist in any mode of being! For it is
the absolute maximum of every rational desire, than
which a greater cannot be.[11]

Focusing on relationship with God will deliver us from
every kind of bondage that has deceived us into pursuing fulfillment in anything that cannot meet the deepest needs of our
nature. It will bring us into revelation of the divine destiny for
our personal lives that only God can reveal and without which
we can never be satisfied. God's DNA for every living soul He
has created can only develop as we personally come into
union with the will of God that He ordained for us. True intimacy with God will satisfy our hearts and bring us to the place
of rest our souls long to find.

CHAPTER 5

In Search of

Rest

Taking Jesus' Yoke

*Come unto me, all ye that labor and are heavy laden,
and I will give you rest.*
—Matthew 11:28

Burnout—that all-inclusive term that has come to mean physical, emotional, and psychological exhaustion resulting in our inability to function effectively in life—may be a seventies' phrase, but it is a present-day reality for many weary souls. In a nation that boasts the shortest work week in history, in a culture that spends more money for leisure and recreation than ever before, millions of Americans complain that they are suffering from exhaustion.

"Couch potatoes" who watch TV an average of more than forty hours a week complain that they are too tired to go to work. Many seek over-the-counter solutions, and a growing number of people are dependent on tranquilizers and sleeping pills, not to mention alcohol and other drugs. Others turn to exercise and diet to seek relief from syndromes of stress and fatigue, a more reasonable answer to the problem at least. How many of us suffer from toxic overload from overindulging on a regular basis, causing physical exhaustion and other distressing physical symptoms?

Psychiatrists, therapists, psychologists, and even psychics are attempting to help people cope with stress. They spend hours with their patients analyzing fears, attitudes, chemical imbalances, or even astrological signs to find solutions to physical and psychological distress. It is evident that people are willing to pay enormous sums of money to anyone who can give them hope of experiencing life without suffering the pangs of emotional and psychological turmoil.

What is the source of our anxiety, stress, exhaustion—our *unrest*? Is it presumptuous to think our psychological woes have a common cause? Surely in our sophisticated world there are many different causes for personal, mental, and emotional distress. Every person responds differently even in the same situations, crises, and environmental factors. What part does our cultural background, our heredity, our upbringing, our physical and mental health, play in our adult emotional responses to life?

"COME UNTO ME"

It was Jesus who declared indiscriminately to a group of people that if they would come to Him, He would give them rest for their souls. Without regard to background, symptoms, or causes of unrest, He issues a promise that seems almost too good to be true:

> Come unto me, all ye that labor and are heavy laden, and I will give you rest. Take my yoke upon you, and learn of me; for I am meek and lowly in heart: and ye shall find rest unto your souls. For my yoke is easy, and my burden is light.
>
> —MATTHEW 11:28–30

A. W. Tozer comments on these verses:

> Here we have two things standing in contrast to each

74

other, a burden and a rest. The burden is not a local one, peculiar to those first hearers, but one which is borne by the whole human race. It consists not of political oppression or poverty or hard work. It is far deeper than that. It is felt by the rich as well as the poor, for it is something from which wealth and idleness can never deliver us. The burden borne by mankind is a heavy and a crushing thing. The word Jesus used means "a load carried or toil borne to the point of exhaustion." Rest is simply release from that burden. It is not something we do; it is what comes to us when we cease to do. His own meekness, that is the rest.[12]

Having been raised in an evangelical environment, I heard these verses quoted many times when those who did not know Christ as their Savior were being invited to come to Him to be born again and experience salvation. As we discussed in an earlier chapter, there is no possibility of knowing peace of mind and heart until we initiate a relationship with the Prince of Peace, Jesus Christ. It is that reconciliation of our life to God in the rebirth experience, becoming new creatures in Christ Jesus, that gives us hope of enjoying the peace that He came to give us.

Yet, while Jesus' words certainly do apply to the burdened heart who has not known the wonderful peace of reconciliation with God and release from the burden of sin, they apply also to the Christian who finds himself laboring under other burdens. Tozer describes the burden Jesus referred to as our pride that is continually offended, our pretense that tries to be better than we are, and our artificiality that creates tension out of fear of discovery.[13] Only the meekness of Jesus, who does not fret over men's response to Him, and who is genuinely loving and humble, can set us free from this crushing burden of our souls and give us the rest we need.

As a Christian, serving God in the areas of children and youth ministry, missions, and music, I have suffered from emotional and physical exhaustion on several occasions. Each time I had to make a dramatic change in my personal lifestyle and ministry situation. It took months of relative inactivity to recover my emotional and physical strength before I could even consider "working for the Lord" in another area of ministry. During my times of exhaustion I struggled with feelings of failure and resentment that I had been used by others to attain their goals. It is self-defeating to feel that someone else has been in charge of your energies and is to blame for your present burned-out condition.

Of course, I had to admit that I *agreed* to someone else's being in charge. It was my own pride and desire to please men that kept me going, doing even more than anyone else required of me. It was during one of my burned-out seasons that I heard these wonderful words of Jesus breathed quietly into my spirit: "Come unto Me, all ye that labor and are heavy laden, and I will give you rest." I knew I needed rest, not just from my labors, but from the burden of false responsibility and personal pride that demanded from me more than I could give.

When Jesus issued His too-good-to-be-true promise of rest for our souls, He was asking us to let Him be in charge of our physical, emotional, and psychological energies. Bringing to Him all the driving forces within us, which are constantly vying for fulfillment, will result in quieting our souls under His wonderful influence. He said He would *give* us rest and then followed immediately by saying we would *find* rest in His presence.

Jesus invites us to come to Him. He promises to give us the rest that we need on every level—physical, psychological, and spiritual. *Rest*—that healthy state of being that is so scarce that it carries a high premium for psychiatrists, therapists, pharmacists, and even recreational businesses who promise it—can only be found in the arms of Jesus. I have seen myself like a crying, frustrated child who, playing in the heat of the day, has been rejected by her friends and comes running into the house. There she buries her dirty, sweaty face in her mother's lap where she finds acceptance, relief, and comfort in her caresses. In that same way I have come to Jesus with my adult frustrations and tears to find His comfort and acceptance. And

I have found His comfort to be more real, more penetrating and lasting, than that of any human relationship.

Of course, Jesus' promise of rest is conditional. We must *choose* to come to Him. Coming to Jesus involves more than simply being born again and then asking Him for occasional help. He was clear concerning the conditions of His promise: "Take my yoke upon you, and learn of me . . ." (Matt. 11:29). Perhaps the picture of taking a yoke is foreign to many of us who have been raised in American suburbia. A yoke, however, was very familiar to Jesus' audience.

A yoke is a wooden apparatus worn by two oxen as they walk side by side. It gives the control of their going and stopping and of the direction in which they go to their master. If it fits comfortably, the yoke is not a bother to the animal; it simply keeps it in touch with its master's desires for its movements. Taking Jesus' yoke upon us gives Him complete control of the direction of our lives. Jesus promised us that His yoke is *easy*, that it is *comfortable*, not difficult to be worn. As we "learn of Him," getting to know His desires for the direction of our lives and *yielding* to them without resistance, we will find rest for our souls.

If we do not choose to come to Jesus, take His yoke, and learn of Him, we automatically come under the tyrannical influence, or yoke, of our own drives, the desires of others, and the designs of Satan. These yokes are the primary cause of our unrest. Even as Christians, if we are driven by our desires to please people or have their acceptance, those desires will become an unbearable yoke, jerking us in this direction and that, resulting in burnout or worse. Even natural and good, drives such as the drive for success or relationship with God and people, are still just that—*drives*—which, if left under our control and the control of others, will condemn us to the cruel unrest that plagues so many Christians.

Ill-fitting yokes rub sore places on an animal's neck and shoulders, making every step, even in obedience, a painful agony. Some sincere Christians who have even discovered their sense of destiny have, nevertheless, failed to *come* to

The Satisfied Heart

Jesus and *learn* of Him in such a way that He can give them His rest, even in their godly pursuits. When they become victims of mental, emotional, and physical breakdown, they often suffer pangs of guilt for failing to achieve their God-given goals. Though they had grasped the purpose of God for their lives, they did not understand that in order to fulfill that purpose, they had to be securely yoked to Jesus, continually moving under His influence, learning of Him.

King Solomon referred to this place of rest when he taught his son:

> Trust in the LORD with all thine heart; and lean not unto thine own understanding. In all thy ways acknowledge him, and he shall direct thy paths. Be not wise in thine own eyes: fear the LORD, and depart from evil. It shall be health to thy navel, and marrow to thy bones.
>
> —PROVERBS 3:5–8

What medical science has only recently discovered regarding our health as it relates to bone marrow, this wise man alluded to thousands of years ago. Health to the very marrow of our bones, the source of life-giving blood, comes from our trusting God and allowing Him to direct our paths. Solomon cautioned his son not to trust in his own self-confidence, but in the Lord, if he wanted to enjoy physical health. We dare not trust the yoke of our own understanding but instead learn to trust all our ways to God and expect Him to direct our paths. How can we expect to enjoy health—mental, emotional, and physical—without taking responsibility to talk to God about everything in our lives and to submit to His guidance? To not do so would be like asking for a prescription of antibiotics for an infection and then expecting to be cured without taking the medicine.

It is wonderful to know that Jesus came to give us rest. By a simple choice to come to Him and learn of Him, we can be delivered from all kinds of yokes that bring distress to our souls. Though there are conditions to enjoying this rest, they are not difficult or expensive, nor do they exclude anyone because of culture, background, age, or economic status. Simply obeying His invitation to come to Him, completely and continually, with everything in our lives, will allow us to enjoy the fulfillment of the promise of learning of Him and finding His rest.

SUPERNATURAL RENEWAL

Cease striving and know that I am God.
—PSALM 46:10, NAS

When we choose to quiet ourselves and wait on God, the psalmist declares that we will know God. As long as we are striving to accomplish our plans and desires, we cannot cultivate that quiet waiting on God that brings a wonderful revelation of Him to our lives. Striving for the approval of men or for a perfect marriage or even to build a great work for God, we will miss the wonderful revelation of God's destiny for our lives revealed in our quiet waiting on Him. We do not yet understand that it is in rest—ceasing from our frenzied activity and human efforts—that we will find the satisfaction that we are seeking in so many other places.

During the recent spiritual renewal that many Christians have been experiencing, the presence of God seemingly overwhelms our bodies with His power and love as we are prayed for and "slain" in the spirit. One evening I was lying on the church carpet enjoying this divine phenomenon, when I experienced a supernatural rest that I had never known before. As I lay there, I was bathed in the presence of God. In His wonderful presence I felt a cessation of all mental and emotional conflict. I experienced release from negative emotional feelings of anxiety, fear, insecurity, anger, and sadness.

At first I wondered if I was still breathing, or if I needed to. Lying there, I thought, *This must be what heaven is like.* All was well with my soul. I felt a complete acceptance by God Himself that wiped away any sense of failure from my own mind or from the projection of others' unhappiness with my performance. I did not want those blissful moments to end. For several days after that experience, I felt that heavenly supernatural rest. Even as I went about my work and normal activities, I felt a detachment from them and a nearness of the presence of God that took all striving and fretting out of my mind. I did not want anyone or anything to disturb that restful state.

I believe that place of emotional and psychological rest exists for us to enjoy on a continual basis in everyday life. As we continue to yield our lives to Jesus and acknowledge Him in all our ways, we will find the conflicts of our souls resolved, even without understanding how it happened. That doesn't mean we will not suffer loss or pain or grief in this life. But when we do, we take the pain to Jesus where we will find rest for our souls. He initiated the wonderful reality of rest from the beginning and is restoring us to His desire for the Sabbath rest.

THE SABBATH REST

> Blessed is the man who keepeth the sabbath from polluting it.
>
> —ISAIAH 56:2

God established a law and a pattern in creation, creating everything in six days and resting on the seventh day. He invoked that law on mankind, making it one of the ten commandments that He gave to Moses: "Remember the sabbath day, to keep it holy" (Exod. 20:8). As with everything else that God ever did, He gave this commandment for a purpose, with a promise for our well-being. We cannot break it without paying the consequences for forfeiting His purpose for Sabbath rest.

For those who say that keeping the Sabbath is adhering to Old Testament law when we are living in New Testament grace, we need to remind them that Jesus came to *fulfill* the law, not to *abolish* it. Those who use that reasoning to pollute the Sabbath would probably not be so quick to violate other of the ten commandments, such as "Thou shalt not kill" or "Thou shalt not commit adultery."

While I do not intend to discuss the differing views of whether the sabbath is Saturday or Sunday, or another day of the week, I do need to establish that Scripture teaches us to observe a Sabbath—a day of rest. While we live different lifestyles from our ancestors, who observed the Sabbath strictly by attending church and rocking on the porch for the rest of the Sabbath, not cooking or doing chores, we still need to allow the Word of God to guide today so that we do not violate the spirit of this commandment. If we conform to the ungodly pattern of our present-day American culture, we will inevitably violate the day of Sabbath rest commanded by God.

COMMANDMENT WITH PROMISE

I do not believe that I will ever understand the deepest reasons for, or meanings of, any of God's commandments. But because I understand that God is love, as I learn to trust His character, I will obey His commandments, knowing they will result in my personal good. God's commandments come with wonderful promises for those who choose to obey them—as well as terrible consequences for those who do not. The Scriptures are filled with wonderful promises to those who keep the Sabbath as He has commanded:

> For thus says the LORD, To the eunuchs who keep My sabbaths, and choose what pleases Me, and hold fast My covenant, to them I will give in My house and within My walls a memorial, and a name better than that of sons and daughters; I will give them an everlasting name which will not be cut off . . . . every one who keeps from profaning the sabbath, and holds fast My covenant; even those I will bring to My holy mountain, and make them joyful in My house of prayer. Their burnt offerings and their sacrifices will be acceptable on My altar; for My

house will be called a house of prayer for all the peoples.
—Isaiah 56:4–7, NAS

God speaks very specifically regarding the Sabbath through His prophet Isaiah. First God gives eunuchs who keep the Sabbath a wonderful promise. Eunuchs were men who had remained single for various reasons. Jesus said, "For there are eunuchs who were born that way from their mother's womb; and there are eunuchs who were made eunuchs by men; and there are also eunuchs who made themselves eunuchs for the sake of the kingdom of heaven" (Matt. 19:12, NAS).

Whatever their reason for remaining single, God's Word promises the single person a memorial and an everlasting name that is more valuable than the heritage of sons and daughters. He declares that their sacrifices are pleasing to Him and promises them a special place in His house of prayer for all nations. What honor and eternal destiny He reserves for single people who simply obey His command to honor the Sabbath.

Keeping the Sabbath is not a command just for eunuchs, however. It is all-inclusive and filled with promise for all who will obey it. Everyone who keeps the Sabbath He will bring to His holy mountain—into His presence—and give them His joy, allowing them to be a part of harvesting the nations. Jesus promised that *all* who came to Him to learn of Him would find rest for their souls (Matt. 11:29).

Even without understanding all God's reasons for commanding a Sabbath rest, we can enjoy the promises that are ours by observing it. Having a meaningful part in the building of the kingdom of God through prayer—that life-changing relationship of intimate communion with God—is certainly worth the discipline of learning to keep a Sabbath holy.

ENJOYING THE SPIRITUAL SABBATH

There is another dimension of Sabbath rest that goes beyond the natural one we are commanded to keep as a day of rest. The New Testament Scriptures relate the sad end of the children of Israel who died in the wilderness because of their refusal to enter into the Sabbath rest of God. The writer to the Hebrews seems to equate that Sabbath rest with our faith, with reference to an "evil, unbelieving heart" that falls away from the living God (Heb. 3:12, NAS). He admonishes all believers:

> Therefore, let us fear lest, while a promise remains of entering His rest, any one of you should seem to have come short of it. For indeed we have had good news preached to us, just as they also; but the word they heard did not profit them, because it was not united by faith in those who heard. For we who have believed enter that rest, just as He has said, "As I swore in My wrath, they shall not enter My rest. . . ." Since therefore it remains for some to enter it, and those who formerly had good news preached to them failed to enter because of disobedience . . .
>
> —HEBREWS 4:1–3, 6, NAS

The heart rest that we crave will be found as a result of our obedience through faith to the commandments of God. The true Sabbath is a supernatural rest to our natural being that can only be found in God. How much weariness of body, mind, and spirit is caused by our lack of faith and our disobedience, knowingly or unknowingly, to the commands of God? The writer to the Hebrews goes on to say:

> Let us therefore be diligent to enter that rest, lest anyone fall through following the same example [the children of Israel] of disobedience.
>
> —HEBREWS 4:11, NAS

He then instructs us that it is the Word of God that is able to guide us into this rest:

> For the word of God is living and active and sharper than any two-edged sword, and piercing as far as the division of soul and spirit, of both joints and marrow,

> and able to judge the thoughts and intentions of the heart. And there is no creature hidden from His sight, but all things are open and laid bare to the eyes of Him with whom we have to do.
>
> —HEBREWS 4:12–13, NAS

I have read this passage many times and winced at the thought of a sword piercing and dividing asunder between my soul and spirit and judging my thoughts and the intentions of my heart. It seems so violent somehow, so graphic, and so sure to cause pain. But my experience of the cleansing power of God's Word to liberate me from my self-destructions has been so wonderful that, though there is pain sometimes involved, it is not long remembered because of the glorious liberty I enjoyed afterward.

Faith comes, according to the Scriptures, by hearing the Word of God (Rom. 10:17). As we are diligent in receiving the Word of God, we will experience its power to cleanse us from our unbelief and bring us into the Sabbath rest of God. The power of the Word to open our eyes to our sin and to the deceptions we have believed will uncover the bondages that have kept us from knowing His rest.

True rest is not possible as long as there is a cover-up—a hiding of our deepest heart desires and motivations. This is true in human relationship as well as in our relationship with God. It is the openness of being known without fear of rejection or condemnation that brings ultimate rest to the soul. That trust has to be cultivated in relationship with God as well as in human relationships and is vital to the rest of our souls. God's Word promises to give us that rest, cutting out the unbelief and other destructive elements that would keep us from it. Through our faith and obedience to His Word, we can receive His promise of a supernatural Sabbath rest which He intended for mankind from the beginning of time.

THE REST IN JESUS' LIFE

Jesus was never threatened by burnout. He completed His

divine mission perfectly by yielding completely to the will of the Father. Waiting quietly in the Father's presence during whole nights of prayer, He kept the communication open between them that insured His perfect obedience to the Father's will. Jesus did not live emotionless, walking dutifully through life to fulfill the will of the Father. Jesus was motivated by love for His Father and strengthened by the communion of that intimate relationship. He offered His disciples His peace, His joy, His abundant life. And He endured even the cross for the joy that was set before Him (Heb. 12:2).

I have had to ask myself many times what has been my motivation for getting involved in a seemingly good work, since it did not produce the fruit I thought it would and seemed to backlash against my physical and emotional well-being. Waiting on God and allowing His Word to do its redemptive work in us is the only way we can insure that even our godly pursuits will have divine approval and be truly successful.

Coming unto Jesus is a continual process and pattern for living—it should characterize our lifestyle as Christians. As each area of our lives comes under the scrutiny of the Word of God and His lordship, our souls as well as our bodies will be delivered from the distresses of unrest that lead to burnout. Taking His yoke and learning of Him, following His declared plan for us in His Word, His specific plan for our lives as revealed to our spirits, will keep us on a glorious pathway to abundant life. By faith, we will enter into His promised Sabbath rest.

There is no greater thrill to me than to hear the Holy Spirit whisper just a phrase or a sentence into my spirit, giving me direction, comfort, or strength for the task at hand. We do live by every word that proceeds out of the mouth of God (Matt. 4:4). As our faith in His Word and our obedience to it increases, so does our rest. And we can look forward to a life of productivity with eternal rewards.

CHAPTER 6

In Search of

Reward

Discovering Divine Recompense

With good will render service, as to the LORD, and not to men, knowing that whatever good thing each one does, this he will receive back from the LORD, whether slave or free.

—Ephesians 6:7–8, NAS

Need a raise? Looking for job satisfaction? Feeling used or useless? Perhaps the reason for your discontent in the home or in the workplace is that you are looking to the wrong source for the reward of your labors. Your employer, spouse, kids, friends, peers—none of these significant relationships are the true source of our remuneration. We should not look to them for our reward, whether financial reimbursement, emotional satisfaction, or psychological affirmation, for a job well done.

According to the Scriptures it is the Lord who recompenses "every man according to his work" (Ps. 62:12). This promise is repeated over and over almost word for word in both the Old and New Testaments.[14] Both Old Testament and New Testament saints knew they were accountable to God alone, who would recompense them for their deeds. Jesus, prophesying

87

of His Second Coming, referred to this reality as well: " For the Son of Man is going to come in the glory of His Father with His angels; and will then recompense every man according to his deeds" (Matt. 16:27, NAS). Though He referred to future recompense, Scriptures also teach the reality of present recompense. The psalmist declared: "The LORD has rewarded me according to my righteousness; according to the cleanness of my hands He has recompensed me" (Ps. 18:20, NAS).

How would our lives change if we received this truth and began to look to God as our employer? Whether we spend our days in the workplace or in the home, making ourselves accountable to God in our employment will make His promise of divine recompense a reality in our lives. In this way we will be able to enjoy the quality of eternal life that He came to give. As we learn to hear His voice we will receive His wisdom for critical decisions. At times, we will be able to sense a divine restraint that will keep us from making wrong choices as we become sensitive to what is not pleasing to Him.

As I have grasped in faith God's promise to recompense me according to my work, I have experienced miraculous changes in my job satisfaction as well as in my financial status. Through a process of learning to "acknowledge the LORD in all my ways," including employment decisions, quality of work, attitudes, and every detail related to my work life, I have found true satisfaction in my work. I simply began to look to the Lord as my employer. I asked Him for wisdom in my tasks as well as financial remuneration according to what He felt was just for my labors. And I became accountable to Him with my attitudes toward my work, my employer, and fellow employees.

Over the past five years of applying this biblical principle of divine recompense in my employment situation, I have moved from a financially liable position to one that is comfortable. The Lord has given me a very positive Christian work environment, which involves a wonderful sense of purpose and allows for personal and professional growth. The more convinced I became of this scriptural promise for divine recompense, the more satisfied I felt at the end of a day, having done my best for my employer, the Lord Himself.

The psalmist declared this truth of divine recompense, not so much as a promise, but as a statement of fact: "And lovingkindness is Thine, O LORD, for Thou dost recompense a man according to his work" (Ps. 62:12, NAS). He had learned from his own experience how God rewards those who serve Him. The word *recompense* in the Hebrew includes these wonderful concepts: "safety, prosperity, fullness, restoration, reward, completion." It refers to more than just financial gain. *Recompense* indicates that the man (or woman) whose life God rewards for work well done is filled with prosperity. God safeguards him (or her) from destruction and fills the person with a sense of completion and satisfaction.

One of my favorite Bible characters is Joseph, the next to youngest son of Jacob. Though he was sold by his brothers into slavery, his life is evaluated in Scriptures the following way: "And the LORD was with Joseph, so he became a successful man" (Gen. 39:2, NAS). Later, when Joseph's character was maligned by his master's seductive wife and he was thrown into prison, the Scriptures again record: "But the LORD was with Joseph . . . and gave him favor in the sight of the chief jailer. . . .because the LORD was with him; and whatever he did, the LORD made to prosper" (Gen. 39:21–23, NAS). Even in hostile circumstances, when the Lord is with us, people will observe the blessing of the Lord on our lives if we choose to acknowledge Him first in all we do.

Perhaps we are aware of this promise for divine recompense but we think it only applies to people who are "full-time" ministers, looking to God by faith for their financial support. That cannot be the case because our modern-day clergy-laity distinction was nonexistent in Bible days. This promise of divine recompense found in both Old and New Testaments was given to everyone who loves God and desires to serve Him.

In their epic book, *Boundaries,* in which Henry Cloud and

The Satisfied Heart

John Townsend beautifully define godly relationships based on biblical principles, they address this issue of accountability in employment:

> Christians often have a warped way of looking at work. Unless someone is working "in the ministry," they see his work as secular. However, this view of work distorts the biblical picture. . . . Wherever we work, whatever we do, we are to do "unto the LORD" (Col. 3:23).
>
> Jesus used parables about work to teach us how to grow spiritually. These parables deal with money, with completing tasks, with faithful stewardship of a job, and with honest emotional dealings in work. They all teach character development in the context of relating to God and others. They teach a work ethic based on love under God.
>
> Work is a spiritual activity. In our work, we are made in the image of God, who is himself a worker, a manager, a creator, a developer, a steward, and a healer. To be a Christian is to be a co-laborer with God in the community of humanity. By giving to others we find true fulfillment. The New Testament teaches that jobs offer more than temporal fulfillment and rewards on earth. Work is the place to develop our character in preparation for the work that we will do forever.[15]

Have you considered your work to be a spiritual activity? Even full-time ministers sometimes categorize their work, feeling that preaching, for example, is spiritual, while answering correspondence and attending to other administrative duties are not. God has commanded us to do everything we do for His glory. That makes everything of spiritual, eternal value, even the most mundane of tasks. What a liberating truth—to think that every ounce of energy we expend can work toward divine recompense if we do it with the right motivation.

If we simply get up one more day to get to work reasonably

on time, do as much as we have to do in order to avoid reprimand, and anxiously watch the clock for the next moments of escape, we have failed to realize the high calling of God in our employment situation. And we will be sure to miss opportunities to be co-laborers with God either as a verbal witness to His goodness or a silent witness as a godly servant.

Oswald Chambers writes of our attitude toward service:

> Paul's idea of service is the same as Our LORD's: "I am among you as He that serveth;" "ourselves your servants for Jesus' sake." We have the idea that a man called to the ministry is called to be a different kind of being from other men. According to Jesus Christ, he is called to be the "doormat" of other men; their spiritual leader, but never their superior. . . .This is Paul's idea of service—"I will spend myself to the last ebb for you; you may give me praise or give me blame, it will make no difference. So long as there is a human being who does not know Jesus Christ, I am his debtor to serve him until he does. The mainspring of Paul's service is not love for men, but love for Jesus Christ. . . .If our motive is love to God, no ingratitude can hinder us from serving our fellow men.[16]

Through our labors, however menial, we are expending our energies in the earth as ambassadors of Christ to reveal the love of God to the world. To love God and become His servant, motivated to serve others, reveals the heart of God who will, by His very nature, have to give to us in return. If that is our true motivation, we can expect to receive wonderful reward from the hand of God Himself.

Jesus is into rewards. He declared: "He who receives a prophet in the name of a prophet shall receive a prophet's reward; and he who receives a righteous man in the name of a righteous man shall receive a righteous man's reward. And whoever in the name of a disciple gives to one of these little ones even a cup of cold water to drink, truly I say to you he shall not lose his reward" (Matt. 10:41–42, NAS). By simply becoming a servant to a man of God, He promises we will receive the same reward that man of God will receive. Whatever small blessing we have to give, He promised, will not go unrewarded.

VIRTUAL REALITY

Looking to God as our source of recompense will deliver us from a place of virtual reality that substitutes our true employer, God, for a human one we have set out to please. Experience has taught me that it is sometimes easier to please God than it is to please some employers. Of course, we should try to satisfy our employers by completing reasonable workloads that are given to us. But, if after the task is satisfactorily completed, our employers withhold approval for a job well done, either through neglect or by intent, we are released from the temptation to feel resentful toward them if we truly learn to look to God for our reward.

As we make ourselves accountable to God, we will not place on our employer an unfair burden to applaud our efforts or build our self esteem. Instead, we are content that we have done our best for God who will ultimately recompense us for our efforts. At the end of a tiring day, we can still experience His rest as we learn to stay in the yoke of employment with Him.

Looking to God for reward also removes the advantage from the unfair employer who uses bully tactics to manipulate employees into unreasonable workloads or other unfair situations. We will have courage to stand against manipulation graciously, being willing to lose a job if necessary rather than be violated by ungodly practices. And if attitudes or verbal assaults become too abusive, we can expect to see the situation improve through our prayer for this unkind employer. If the situation becomes intolerable, we can look to God to place us in a different situation.

Being accountable to God sets us free to expect God's divine recompense including *safety* and *satisfaction* as well as prosperity. When our trust is not in our temporal place of employment but in God who has promised to recompense us according to our work, we do not have to be victims of an unfair employer. God will provide a safe place for us as we look to Him to provide what we need in employment.

I have a friend who worked for a large chemical company among many ungodly men. The competition and unfair put-downs were increased by unfair methods of promotion that were used throughout the plant. My friend was daily harassed by a fellow employee who was "all mouth." His insults and abusive language vexed this Christian man. Finally, he and his wife began to agree in prayer that this situation would change, though it seemed impossible by human calculation.

One day my friend returned home from work with a big grin on his face. He said to his wife, "You will never guess what happened to _____ today."

She looked at her husband curiously, wondering about his big grin. "What happened?" she asked.

"They moved him to another department without even a promotion. No one knows why." But my friend and his wife knew that God had heard their cry.

NEGATIVE RECOMPENSE

Because God is just, He not only rewards those who do well; He also recompenses the evil person for his or her evil deeds. The prophet declared this reality:

> The lips of my assailants and their whispering are against me all day long. Look on their sitting and their rising; I am their mocking song. Thou wilt recompense them, O LORD, according to the work of their hands.
> —LAMENTATIONS 3:62–64, NAS

It is a comfort to know that if we do justly we will receive our just recompense from the Lord. It is also wonderful to know that God is aware of injustices that are worked against us, and He will repay those who are responsible. We are truly safe in the hands of God if we determine to make the right choices to please Him in all we do.

We must also be warned to expect God's negative response to us if we do not choose to live godly lives in the workplace and allow Him to change our character. The prophet continues to describe the recompense the evil person can expect:

> Thou wilt give them hardness of heart, Thy curse will be on them. Thou wilt pursue them in anger and destroy them from under the heavens of the LORD!
> —LAMENTATIONS 3:65–66, NAS

Hardness of heart is a fearful state to contemplate. If we allow hardness of heart because of one sin, it will affect our lives in every area. Giving place to hatred toward one person, for example, opens the door to that vile sin of indiscriminate hatred. Allowed to grow in our hearts, hatred will contaminate all of our relationships with its venom. Sin is destructive, and the goal of sin is to utterly destroy our lives.

For that reason the Scriptures admonish us: "Watch over your heart with all diligence, for from it flow the springs of life" (Prov. 4:23, NAS). If we choose to harden our hearts as we go through hurtful situations in life, we will be the losers. Instead, we need to take every hurt to God and receive His healing balm through forgiveness and, if need be, repentance, allowing Him to wash and cleanse our hearts so we can continue to live a life that is pleasing to Him in all we do. David cried out for this wonderful power of cleansing after his moral failure:

> Purify me with hyssop, and I shall be clean; wash me, and I shall be whiter than snow. . . .Create in me a clean heart, O God, and renew a steadfast spirit within me.
> —PSALM 51:7,10, NAS

It is not possible to live daily in the "marketplace" or in the home without at times suffering a sense of violation from peers, superiors, friends, and even family. Sometimes the seemingly little disappointments and frustrations are the most hurtful — those things that are not life threatening but reveal a lack of caring or concern toward our personal needs.

Someone has said that the problem with life is that it is so daily. I have coined the phrase: "Life can be bratty." You know, like a child who is uncooperative, interruptive, messy—not evil or destructive, just bratty. In reality, we are accountable to God alone in these seemingly insignificant tests that reveal our motivation and character. That is when it is important to know that He is the One to whom we look, by faith, for our recompense.

Jesus said to a group of Jews, "How can you believe, when you receive glory from one another, and you do not seek the glory that is from the one and only God?" (John 5:44, NAS). He knew they were more interested in what others said about them than about finding the truth—who was standing in their midst. The Greek word for *glory* used by Jesus in His reprimand to the Jews means "dignity, honor, praise, and worship." The motivation for everything they did was to heap honor, praise, and even worship upon themselves.

These Jews were living in the virtual reality of receiving from men honor that counterfeited the real glory God would have given them. This wrong motivation rendered them helpless to believe in the Christ who stood before them. Jesus declared that they did not even believe in Moses, for if they had they would have believed in Jesus as well. We can conclude that their wrong motivation affected their faith adversely. Because they looked to men for honor and praise, they could not believe in Christ.

Our search for reward and approval, so basic to mankind, must be redirected toward receiving the approval of God if we ever want to find true fulfillment in our work. We can even be used of God in powerful ministry situations without ever experiencing heart satisfaction if our motivation is not correct. Jesus confirmed this stark reality:

> So then, you will know them by their fruits. Not
> every one who says to Me, "LORD, LORD," will enter the

kingdom of heaven; but he who does the will of My Father who is in heaven. Many will say to Me on that day, "LORD, LORD, did we not prophesy in Your name, and in Your name cast out demons, and in Your name perform many miracles?" And then I will declare to them, "I never knew you; depart from Me, you who practice lawlessness."

—MATTHEW 7:20–23, NAS

Having been raised in a minister's home and then preparing myself for the ministry in a classic educational environment, I found these verses to be almost too radical to handle. How could one who casts out devils and works miracles in the name of Jesus be accused of lawlessness (iniquity)? We were taught that the higher you went in God the more power you had against the enemy. And a "miracle worker" was about as good as it gets. Yet Jesus was telling these people who prophesied and worked miracles that He never knew them.

The word translated *know* in the Greek is a comprehensive term for "intimate knowledge that comes only through relationship." It does not refer to a casual acquaintance, but rather to knowing a person by virtue of having intimate relationship with him. According to Jesus' perspective of Christianity, unless He has that intimate relationship with a person, He regards all that person does as lawless—iniquitous. It is sobering to realize that holiness is really all God is interested in.

REWARD OF HOLINESS

The prophet Isaiah proclaimed a wonderful prophecy to those who were expecting the salvation of God:

Say to the daughter of Zion, "Lo, your salvation comes; behold His reward is with Him, and His recompense before Him." And they will call them, "The holy people, the redeemed of the LORD"; and you will be called, "Sought out, a city not forsaken."

—ISAIAH 62:11–12, NAS

Holiness is not some perfect state of virtue to which we try to attain through years of constant striving and continual disappointment. According to the prophet, holiness is the reward of the Lord, His recompense to the redeemed. As we focus our attention on God, seeking to please Him, He will become our holiness. Until we grasp by faith the eternal reality that Christ is our life—our wisdom, our righteousness, our sanctification, our redemption (1 Cor. 1:30)—we will never enjoy the reward of holiness. We are incapable of true holiness apart from intimate relationship with Christ.

The word *holy* translated here means "consecrated, dedicated, hallowed." In order to experience true holiness, our part is simply to *choose* to consecrate ourselves to the Lordship of Christ and to walk in dependence on Him, acknowledging Him in all our ways. He will show us the path of holiness with all its rewards—freedom from the ravaging power of sin, direction into the purposes of God, and deliverance from the wrong motivation of seeking the approval of others.

Such a blissful life will be sought out by others who see the beauty of peace in adversity, joy in sorrow, and righteousness in the face of temptation. They will know that we have relationship with Someone who is helping us to be victorious in all of life's situations. And they will want to know the Christ who is shining through our lives.

The apostle Paul wrote to the Roman Christians, "But now being made free from sin, and become servants to God, ye have your fruit unto holiness, and the end everlasting life (Rom. 6:22). A more clear translation states: "But now having been freed from sin and enslaved to God, you derive your benefit, resulting in sanctification, and the outcome, eternal life" (NAS). The benefit of becoming "enslaved" to Christ is to be free from sin, resulting in holiness and all that it provides for our lives now and in eternity. Though most of my concern is how to live life in the nasty here and now, I take great comfort in knowing that how I live life today will affect me for eternity.

FUTURE REWARD

For the Son of Man is going to come in the glory of
His Father with His angels; and will then recompense
every man according to his deeds.

—MATTHEW 16:27

Eternity is forever. It stretches my imagination to the max
to meditate on timelessness—when time will no longer have
meaning to us. Even our vocabulary is unfit for such thoughts.
We cannot discuss eternity without contrasting it with time,
for that is all we have known. We use such phrases as, "There
will be no more time," or, "After the first thousand years I
want to. . . ." But assigning vast amounts of time to stretch our
thinking does not place us in eternity—it only increases our
sense of captivity to time.

Eternity is past, present, and future (another time-relevant
description.) Jesus taught that eternal life was knowing God. I
believe that to the degree we come to know God on earth, the
restrictions of time are lifted from our hearts and minds, and
we relate more to eternity than anything else.

That doesn't mean that I do not have to be at work on time
or be required to meet a publisher's deadline. But the perspective we have from eternity puts earthly things into a different
light and makes them of lesser priority. We are more concerned about pleasing our eternal Father than in having the
approval of men, for example. Eternal life is a quality of life
that liberates us from the flesh bondages of arbitrary personal
demands and the demands of others. They simply are not as
important as they used to be.

A few years ago when my father suffered a massive stroke
that took his life, a dear friend offered to take me to the airport
to go be with my family. She shared with me later that as we
said good-bye that day, God spoke to her these words, "I am
putting eternity into her heart." The loss of my father is the
greatest emotional loss I have suffered. Yet to have the assur-
ance that this godly man is resting in a heavenly place in the

presence of God has indeed made me wistful at times to be with him. I have focused much more on eternal values, evaluating the ways I spend my time so they will have eternal significance for my life and the lives of others, and making sure my heart attitudes are right before God. And I have spent more time contemplating eternity itself.

It is God's will to put eternity into our hearts. All of life is a proving ground for that reality. As we allow holiness to work true motivation in us so that we may bring glory to God in all we do, we can find true fulfillment in our search for recompense. Whether we consider present financial, psychological, emotional, or spiritual rewards or contemplate future rewards, if we make ourselves accountable to God we will be assured of finding true fulfillment in our search for recompense. And our search will inevitably lead us to a deeper encounter with Wisdom—the Son of God Himself.

CHAPTER 7

In Search of

Wisdom

Eating the Living Word

*When He marked out the foundations of the earth;
then I [Wisdom] was beside Him, as a master
workman; and I was daily His delight, rejoicing
always before Him . . . having my delight in the sons
of men.*

—Proverbs 8:29–31, NAS

The Book of Proverbs personifies wisdom in such a beautiful poetic way, describing, of course, our lovely Savior, Jesus. No one could desire or dream of a greater utopia of happiness or success in life than that which wisdom promises. In order to seize those promises and make them effective for our lives, however, we cannot allow them to remain mere poetry to our ears. Instead we need to determine that we will have what wisdom holds out to us:

> Counsel is mine and sound wisdom; I am under-
> standing, power is mine. By me kings reign, and rulers
> decree justice. By me princes rule, and nobles, all who
> judge rightly. I love those who love me; and those who
> diligently seek me will find me. Riches and honor are

101

with me, enduring wealth and righteousness.
—Proverbs 8:14–18, NAS

Power, justice, love, honor, riches, righteousness—all of these divine qualities of life are promised to the one who seeks God in such a way that he or she finds wisdom. It seems too good to be true. Surely such a quality of life must be reserved for a special few. Can the average person expect to enjoy such a wonderful life as wisdom promises?

MEETING THE CONDITIONS

Though it seems too good to be true, according to the Scriptures, anyone who meets the conditions stated can enjoy the quality of life wisdom offers. All those who seek for wisdom early and diligently will enjoy its divine benefits in this earthly life:

Blessed is the man who listens to me, watching daily at my gates, waiting at my doorposts. For he who finds me finds life, and obtains favor from the LORD.
—Proverbs 8:34–35, NAS

Choosing to diligently seek for wisdom involves watching, waiting and listening at His gates. This is no haphazard lifestyle of *que será será*. It involves a determination to learn the ways of wisdom in order to reap the benefit of the life they offer. Watching, waiting, seeking—not impossible conditions, but conditions nevertheless that must be met in order to find wisdom. We have to *learn* to seek for wisdom. It does not come naturally. Sometimes we only realize our lack of wisdom after our propensity for foolishness has caused us pain and grief. We must also be aware, according to the Scriptures, that those who refuse to seek wisdom will suffer the stated consequences for not doing so: "But he who sins against me injures himself; all those who hate me love death" (Prov. 8:36, NAS).

The Scriptures teach that we are predisposed to foolishness from our childhood: "Foolishness is bound in the heart of a

102

child; but the rod of correction shall drive it far from him" (Prov. 22:15). Proper discipline is necessary for a child to learn to make right choices and to become obedient to the wisdom of godly parents. Children who are taught to obey their parents will sooner seek the ways of wisdom as adults, having benefited from the correction their parents gave them that drove foolishness from their hearts.

As adults, unless we make a conscious decision to seek the wisdom of God for our lives, develop a life of prayer, and consecrate ourselves to obey the Word of God, we will live our lives according to our own self-determination. Our carnal minds are naturally filled with our own opinions, our personal sense of justice, our faulty concepts of love and relationship, and our fierce loyalty to independence which we have developed from early childhood.

King Solomon understood this when he said, "There is a way which seemeth right unto a man; but the end thereof are the ways of death" (Prov. 14:12). Until we repent for going our own way, turning from it to seek the way of wisdom, we will have to suffer the pangs of death that our own way produces in every area of our lives. As we turn from our own way and learn to "wait at the doorposts of wisdom," God's Word promises that we will find life. All that God intended for life to be is found in the house of wisdom.

It is not because the conditions are too difficult or because wisdom's wonderful promises are reserved for a few that we do not receive the power, justice, love, honor, riches, and righteousness to be found in wisdom. The cause of our failure to enjoy the quality of life that wisdom promises is that we do not wholeheartedly seek to know Him. Consciously or unconsciously, we think that our way is right, and we make lifetime decisions and choices according to our own desires without seeking to know the wisdom of the Living Word.

PLAYING THE FOOL

For many years I read the Book of Proverbs from the

perspective of the "wise," applying all the promises recorded for the wise to my life. I was sincerely seeking to know wisdom, studying the Word, and maintaining a fervent devotional life. Yet I wondered why I did not see some of these promises being fulfilled in my life. It was not until I began to consider the *fool* in the Book of Proverbs that I "located" the cause for some of the humiliations I had experienced in life. I had not yet learned to "acknowledge him in all my ways."

That is not to despise the measure of righteousness that is working in me. But when I began to encounter difficulties in personal relationships and to suffer problems of burnout that affected my physical and emotional health, I realized that my ways were leading to death. And, according to the Scriptures, that described the path of the fool, rather than the path of the wise. Because I had assumed the posture of the wise, I had been ensnared by my own foolishness. It is wonderful when light from the Word shines on our ways, exposing our foolishness to ourselves. For then we are able to forsake our foolish ways and embrace the ways of life.

One particular proverb that exposed my foolishness was the one that exhorts us:

> Let your foot rarely be in your neighbor's house, lest
> he become weary of you and hate you.
> —PROVERBS 25:17, NAS

For many years, as a single person, I fled my solitude by practically living in the homes of friends or neighbors. Though I remember reading this proverb many times, I reasoned that it meant something other than what it did. However, I was violating this proverb and suffering the consequences it promises to those who do so. No need to wallow in self-pity and feel like no one loves you when you are the one creating the situation by violation of a simple law of relationship. I made some necessary adjustments in my lifestyle, and my relationships improved over time.

Another scripture that proved painfully true in my life had to do with what I thought was my godly desire for others to have more of God than they evidently wanted for themselves. As director of a young women's rehabilitation center, I agonized over the wrong choices each girl made. Instead of making their decisions a matter of prayer, I spent countless hours counseling and cajoling these girls who "used" my sympathetic responses, draining my emotional reserves. Then one day as I approached the Word from this new posture of the fool, I saw it:

> No man can by any means redeem his brother, or give to God a ransom for him—For the redemption of his soul is costly, and he should cease trying forever.
> —PSALM 49:8, NAS

In the Hebrew, the word *redeem* translated here means to "release, rescue, preserve, and deliver." Only God can redeem a soul in this sense. Feeling helpless to convince my counselees of the wonderful life they could have in God, I realized as I read this verse that I had foolishly tried to rescue them and deliver them *personally* instead of bringing them to Jesus. When I acknowledged that I could not be responsible for their redemption, I was the one who was delivered from a sense of false responsibility that had robbed me of peace, energy, and joy. Of course, counseling can be helpful, but it does not have the redemptive power to save a soul.

The psalmist declared, "Thy Word is a lamp to my feet, and a light to my path" (Ps. 119:105, NAS). As we walk with the Living Word, He is faithful to shine His light on our path and deliver us from all our destructions. Again, the psalmist declared: "He sent His word and healed them, and delivered them from their destructions" (Ps. 107:20, NAS). He will not only heal our bodies, but also our destructive ways, foolish attitudes, and vain pursuits as we seek Him in His Word. We will never know satisfaction apart from seeking and finding wisdom in the person of Christ.

WISDOM IS A PERSON

King Solomon had supernatural insight by the Holy Spirit into the *person* of wisdom as well as the *power* of wisdom. He knew that personal relationship with Wisdom (Jesus) was not only possible, but was absolutely necessary in order to discover life as God intended we should live it. That is why he taught us to lean not on our own understanding but to acknowledge God all our ways (Prov. 3:5–6). We are to live in such close relationship to Wisdom that we do nothing without consulting with Him. And we need to be willing to deny our own understanding in order to obey Him.

Christ is faithful to reveal His wisdom to us if we seek Him. We can expect Him to respond to us in a way we can understand if we are willing and diligent to acknowledge Him in all our ways. Our failure to discover the wisdom we need for our lives is not because He is unwilling to be found. The New Testament declares: "If any of you lack wisdom, let him ask of God, that giveth to all men liberally, and upbraideth not; and it shall be given him" (James 1:5). Without fear of condemnation, we can come to God and ask for the wisdom we lack, and He will give it. In fact, the New Testament teaches that Jesus has become our wisdom (1 Cor. 1:30, AMP).

John was the disciple who received wonderful revelation of who Jesus was in eternity. He began his Gospel by declaring:

> In the beginning was the Word, and the Word was with God, and the Word was God. The same was in the beginning with God. All things were made by him; and without him was not any thing made that was made. In him was life; and the life was the light of men.
>
> —JOHN 1:1–4

As Solomon personified *Wisdom* to describe Jesus, so John personifies the *Word* to describe Him. They declare the Son of God to be both Wisdom and the Word, the power behind all of creation. John had the joy of introducing Jesus to us as the

Word made flesh. God—Wisdom, the Word—became flesh in the incarnation.

THE INCARNATION

Harold Caballeros, pastor of a powerful church in Guatemala, teaches that there is only one will in the universe—the will of God. There are not two wills—a righteous one and a wicked one. God has a will for life as He intended it to be. Anything that opposes that will is only a *usurper* of the will of God, not another will. The devil usurps the will of God, influencing men and women to exercise their free wills against the lordship of Christ. That makes them usurpers as well. To know the *will* of God for our lives, we must know the *Word* of God, who became the Son of God.

The Word of God *is* the will of God. In creation, God *spoke* the worlds into existence. Everything was created by the power of His Word. According to the Scriptures, when the Word became flesh and dwelt among us, we beheld the glory of God (John 1:14). God incarnate in Jesus Christ—Wisdom, the Word, the Son of God.

Can we ever expect to comprehend the greatness of God's love which was willing and able to clothe Himself with human flesh in order that we might come to know Him as the Living Word? I'm convinced that throughout eternity we will be simply catching glimpses of this incomprehensible phenomenon we call the incarnation. Yet as we meditate on this wonder we can receive revelation of God that will change our hearts and bring us into more intimate relationship with Him.

We have mentioned that John records Jesus' prayer in which He defines eternal life for us: "And this is life eternal, that they might know thee the only true God, and Jesus Christ, whom thou hast sent" (John 17:3). To the degree we cultivate relationship with God here on earth we can experience eternal life, which Jesus came to give. Eternal life is that quality of "abundant life" that Jesus declared He had come to give. It sets us free from sin, self, and Satan, and restores relationship with our Creator God.

Everything that Jesus did while He was on earth not only revealed the Father to us, but also revealed to us the eternal, Living Word, who was from the beginning. Surely our priority in life should be to know Him so that we might experience the eternal life He came to give us. Perhaps the apostle Paul describes most clearly the process of the Word becoming flesh. He speaks of the *kenosis* or "emptying" of Christ of all His divine attributes to become man:

> Let this mind be in you, which was also in Christ Jesus: who, being in the form of God, thought it not robbery to be equal with God: but made himself of no reputation, and took upon him the form of a servant, and was made in the likeness of men: and being found in fashion as a man, he humbled himself, and became obedient unto death, even the death of the cross.
>
> —PHILIPPIANS 2:5–8

Have you ever thought that when Christ humbled Himself to become man, He was not coming from a place of exalted pride, but from a legitimate position of equality with God? To reveal the glory of the Father, Christ humbled Himself to take the place of an obedient servant. He was willing to make Himself of no reputation and to become a servant, even to the death of the cross. What a contrast to our situations where we find it extremely painful to humble our proud hearts in order to become servants. Would we choose to make ourselves of no reputation if we had a legitimate claim to position and power as Christ did?

If we are truly seeking Wisdom, we will have to embrace His humbling process for our own lives. In order to recognize Wisdom, we will have to let His mind be in us. Without recognizing Him in His humbling, we will never know Wisdom. And apart from wisdom we will forfeit the promises of life He offers us.

THE BREAD OF LIFE

"I am the bread of life," Jesus declared. "He that cometh to me shall never hunger; and he that believeth on me shall never thirst" (John 6:35). Jesus' declaration startled the people. The Jews asked how Jesus could give them His flesh to eat (v. 52). They did not understand that the bread of heaven would feed their spirits, giving them eternal life. Their eyes were blinded to eternal realities, and they could only think in human, earthly terms.

If their darkened minds could have received the truth of what He was saying, they could have exchanged the spiritual poverty of their religious lives for the living bread He offered them. They did not recognize Jesus as the Living Word who had the power to give them eternal life.

The apostle James instructs us to "receive and welcome the Word which implanted and rooted [in your hearts] *contains the power to save your souls* (James 1:21, AMP, emphasis added). The written Word contains a supernatural power to be implanted and rooted in our hearts, changing us into the image of Christ. As we choose to eat the Word, reading it regularly and prayerfully, and understanding that the power of the Living Word is resident in it, our lives will be continually transformed. We will begin to grasp the significance of the *Word made flesh* and experience the glorious reality of the apostle Paul's declaration: "Christ in you, the hope of glory" (Col. 1:27).

As we receive the written Word of God for what it is—supernatural food to our spirits, which has power to transform our minds, wills, and emotions, we will learn to know Christ as the Living Word. Even without understanding the significance of all the Bible customs or mysteries of the Bible, we can come to the "table" to eat the Word of God as we would come to a smorgasbord of food.

We do not have to understand the botanical makeup of vegetables and fruits lining a lovely buffet in order for them to nourish our bodies. We simply place them into our mouths, chew them, and swallow them. We don't have to understand how protein works in our systems to give us strength. We simply eat it to receive its benefit to our bodies. I believe we can be changed by the Word of God by simply "eating it." And we can trust the Holy Spirit to open our eyes to the revelation of the Word that we do not understand.

We cannot look to any other source for spiritual strength and health for our spirits that will make our lives successful. Only the Word of God is able to save our souls from our own self destructions. Eating it, meditating on it, memorizing it, learning its precepts, and obeying them will guarantee us the wonderful life that Wisdom promises. The Word of God will nourish our spirits and guide us in our search for wisdom.

I am concerned that the Charismatic Movement, with all its wonderful blessings, has inadvertently weakened our personal sense of responsibility to eat the Word for ourselves. There has been such emphasis on the wonderful teaching and ministering gifts that are such a blessing corporately to the body of Christ that I fear some Christians do not expect to receive personal revelation from the Word of God. Rather, they look to their favorite teacher to feed them.

The personal seeking of wisdom through reading the Scriptures and meditating on the law of God has been substituted by some for the spectator role of listening to a good sermon. Though we do receive wonderful blessing, help, and revelation from the preached Word, there is no substitute for our personal reading of the Word. As we give ourselves to the study and meditation of the written Word, we are inevitably drawing near to the Living Word, Christ Himself. He dwells in us and as we behold Him, the Scriptures teach that we are changed into the same image from glory to glory, even as by the Spirit of the Lord (2 Cor. 3:18).

What makes a letter from a loving father so special to the daughter living far away? It is not the particular words on paper that thrill her heart. It is their relationship of love and trust that she and the letter-writer father have cultivated through the years that causes such joy when a letter is received—before it is ever opened. No matter what the letter says, it will be an expression of the love of that father for his daughter, which he has been expressing since her childhood.

The Scriptures are our love letter from our heavenly Father. As we cultivate an intimate relationship with God, loving and obeying His Word, we will understand the meaning of His letters to us more clearly. We develop an appetite for "every word that proceedeth out of the mouth of God" through our relationship with the Living Word (Matt. 4:4). As we learn to know His heart, the fullness of every word will burst into our hearts with new significance, and we will walk in the wisdom of His Word, allowing Him to become our righteousness.

CHAPTER 8

In Search of

Justice

Invoking the Righteous Judge

*I know that the LORD will maintain the cause of the
afflicted, and justice for the poor.*
—Psalm 140:12, NAS

The abused child, the battered wife, the rapist's victim, the
youth paralyzed because of drunk driving—all are filled with
deep emotional outrage because of injustice, having been violated against their wills by another human being. The
employee of thirty-five years who finds himself a victim of
corporate downsizing, the rejected fiancée, and the bullied sibling must also deal with the pain of injustice, trying to find a
way to live at peace with themselves and others.

There are as many injustices endured among humanity as
there are people—more perhaps. And while some, because of
their own warped sense of justice, see themselves as victims of
society, many others are suffering the effects of real injustices
that have violated their humanity. Entire races grapple with the
oppression of a false sense of inferiority and prejudice that a
self-proclaimed superior race has perpetrated against them.

"That's not fair!" screams the two-year-old who has just

been asked to share his toy with his sibling. Where does the outraged cry of the toddler for justice, so familiar to all of us, originate? Where does this innate perception of violation come from? Isn't it presumptuous to expect fairness and justice in the face of the blatant selfishness of the human race? Perhaps we should learn to be more conformed to the small injustices that offend our dignity every day. But what of those overwhelming, destructive injustices we suffer? Can we really expect to find a peaceful resolution to their evil effects?

In the litigation society in which we live, the most bizarre complaints are taken to our court system. People who are determined to seek justice appeal to the court system as the official vehicle for that pursuit. If the plaintiff wins, he or she must be content with a verdict that awards them a sum of money or penalizes their adversary, perhaps through imprisonment. But (without analyzing the effectiveness of the courts), can a person's sense of justice be satisfied—really satisfied—by winning their case in that way? Is that winning, really? Does receiving a monetary settlement or punishing the perpetrator of our injustice satisfy our real cry for justice?

The human psyche has an uncanny ability to perceive injustice. Can it be fooled into thinking that justice has been served through an arbitrary decision by the court? If our answer is *yes*, perhaps we are willing to conform to that superficial concept of justice because we feel we have no other recourse. A court decision in our favor is the best for which we can hope to resolve the feeling of violation to our person.

And though the court system is overloaded with countless victims seeking justice, there are other countless people who do not have even that recourse to resolve their unjust situation. How will they deal with the anger, frustration, violation, murderous thoughts, and depression that result from their injustices? Must they live the rest of their lives despairing of ever experiencing true vindication?

Our answers to these questions depend entirely upon how we learn to relate to a just God. According to the Scriptures,

God loves justice. Over and over we read comforting promises such as these:

> A false balance is abomination to the LORD: but a just weight is his delight.
>
> —PROVERBS 11:1

> For the LORD loves justice, and does not forsake His godly ones.
>
> —PSALM 37:28, NAS

> I will give thanks to the LORD with all my heart; I will tell of all Thy wonders . . . .For Thou hast maintained my just cause; Thou dost sit on the throne judging righteously.
>
> —PSALM 9:1, 4, NAS

Is it possible that God Himself would come into our personal situations and give to us the justice we crave? From the Scriptures as well as the testimonies of many believers, our answer is a resounding YES! We can know God in such a way that He will personally vindicate us and heal us from the ill effects of the wrong treatment we have received, the injustices we have suffered.

JUSTICE DEFINED

Webster's dictionary defines *justice* as the "maintenance or administration of what is just, especially by the impartial adjustment of conflicting claims or the assignment of merited rewards or punishments. It involves conformity to truth, fact, or reason."[17] It is difficult to think that sinful men can arbitrate the claims of one another and bring true justice to a situation. Our courts can only be instruments for justice to the degree that they conform to the truth of God and His Word. Truth for many has become the subjective reasoning of their own perception of justice. Without the absolute standard of God's truth forming the basis for judicial decisions, we have no hope of receiving the true administration of justice to our situations.

The Hebrew word *shaphat* is a primary root that means "to judge or vindicate, litigate, defend, plead, reason, or rule." David used the word *justice,* which comes from this root word, when he declared: "I know that the LORD will maintain the cause of the afflicted, and justice for the poor (Ps. 140:12, NAS). God is into justice. He hates injustice—it is an abomination to Him (Prov. 20:23). He will vindicate and plead our case if we will call on Him to intervene in the personal injustices we have suffered. He will be our judge and will bring a proper verdict for our lives.

When we are born again we begin to experience release from the isolation we suffered because of our separation from our Creator. As we develop relationship with God through reading His Word, we learn that God loves justice. Discovering how He intervened in the lives of biblical characters who suffered injustices and received God's kind vindication, we can learn to receive from Him the justice we seek.

RECEIVING DIVINE JUSTICE

Many of God's heroes who suffered terrible injustices at the hands of people they had trusted were helped by God's divine intervention as they called on Him. Leah, eldest daughter of Laban, suffered rejection from her husband, Jacob, who loved Rachel her younger sister. And David, anointed to be king over Israel by the prophet Samuel, was forced to live in a cave as a fugitive from King Saul, who searched for him for years to kill him. Studying briefly the responses of these biblical characters to their personal injustices will help us to receive God's divine intervention into our own unjust situations.

TAKING SIDES WITH "PLAIN JANE"

Leah, the older sister of Rachel, was given to Jacob as his wife deceitfully by Laban, her father. Jacob loved Rachel and had promised to work seven years for Laban in order to take her as his wife. As custom would not permit a younger daughter to enter into marriage before the eldest daughter, Laban tricked Jacob, covering Leah's face, and presenting her to Jacob as his wife.

The victim in this situation, Leah, did nothing to deserve the prejudicial treatment she received from Jacob, her husband. The Bible says simply that Jacob loved Rachel more than Leah (Gen. 29:30). The bitterness of her soul is difficult for us to imagine. But anyone who has suffered the unfaithfulness of a spouse can relate to the violation she must have felt.

"And when the LORD saw that Leah was hated, he opened her womb: but Rachel was barren" (Gen. 29:31). The fact that God took note of Jacob's hatred for Leah and intervened to bless her by giving her children should give hope to everyone who has suffered injustice from a spouse. God's answer to the injustice Jacob meted to Leah was to give her what every woman craves—He gave her sons. God showed His divine favor on Leah's life by blessing her with children.

Leah bore Jacob four sons, and with the birth of each one, she hoped that Jacob's heart would be turned to her. Though that was not the result, Leah was experiencing the love of God in new ways with each son she bore, as reflected in the names she gave them. Francis Frangipane expresses so clearly Leah's spiritual progress toward God through her painful journey through injustice:

Three times we read in this text that the Lord saw and heard that she [Leah] was unloved. He had seen her affliction. Through all her striving for Jacob and her disappointment with her marital relationship, the Lord was tenderly wooing her to himself.

As Leah became pregnant a fourth time, a miracle of grace occurred within her. She gradually became aware that, while she had not been the focus of her husband's love, she was loved by God. And as this fourth pregnancy drew near to completion, she drew nearer and nearer to God. She became a worshiper of the Almighty.

Now as she gave birth to another son, she said, "This time I will praise the LORD" (v. 35). She named that child *Judah*, which means "praise." It was from the tribe of Judah that Christ was born.

Leah had been seeking self-fulfillment and found only heartache and pain. But as she became a worshiper of God, she entered life's highest fulfillment: *She began to please God. . . .*

As she found fulfillment in God, He began to remove from her the jealousies, insecurities, and heartaches that life had conveyed to her. A true inner beauty started growing in Leah; she became a woman at rest.[18]

It is our progress in God that is most important to each of our lives. As we choose to seek Him, to cry out to Him, God will use even the most negative circumstances of injustice in our lives for our good. When our hearts are finally turned toward God alone, we are freed from the pain that injustice has inflicted upon us. Rather, it becomes only an instrument in the hands of God to bring us to fulfillment we can find only in relationship with God.

DAVID'S FORGIVING HEART

David had suffered terrible injustices at the hands of King Saul, who pursued him without cause to murder him. Though David had served his king well, King Saul's jealousy filled him with hatred for David, and he was determined to kill him. David learned to call on God for his safety and found that God did come to his aid. Many of David's psalms extol God as his rock, his hiding place, his strong tower of safety.

Besides calling on God, David knew that in order to receive divine intervention against his enemies, he had to also demonstrate a righteous heart toward them. When a messenger brought news to him of Saul's death, David inquired as to the messenger's knowledge of the tragedy. When the messenger admitted to aiding in the death of Saul, David had him put to death for touching God's anointed one. (See 2 Samuel 1:1–19.) Then David mourned and wept, tearing his clothes in grief over the death of Saul and his son Jonathan. He chanted his lament, crying "How have the mighty fallen!" (2 Sam. 1:19, NAS).

In Search of *Justice*

This was no politically correct response feigned from David's lips. It was the true response of his righteous heart, which had not allowed him to kill his enemy Saul when he had the chance. David had learned to reverence God more than he feared man. He was known as a man after God's own heart. And God came to David, as he declares:

> He delivered me from my strong enemy, and from those who hated me, for they were too mighty for me. They confronted me in the day of my calamity, but the LORD was my stay. He brought me forth also into a broad place; He rescued me, because He delighted in me. The LORD has rewarded me according to my righteousness; according to the cleanness of my hands He has recompensed me.
>
> —PSALM 18:17–20, NAS

There was no revenge lurking in David's heart against Saul. Though David knew that he was anointed to be the next king over Israel and that King Saul had corrupted himself, he did not try to avenge himself in any way. Even when urged by his men to take the life of Saul when he had the chance, David repented for cutting the corner from the king's garment. Not even in the slightest way did he want to displease God by touching God's anointed king.

While living as a fugitive from his enemy, David continued to do what he could to protect and deliver the people of God. He did not sit in his cave, passively wallowing in self-pity while suffering the injustices of King Saul's jealous hatred. Instead, David actively pursued the enemies of God's people, Israel, on other fronts, while at the same time developing an army of men who would one day become his loyal leaders. His focus was still on the work of the kingdom, though he had to accomplish it during times of danger and duress.

The psalms are filled with the wonderful revelation of God's heart, which David experienced during his years of "personal violation" that forced him to live as an exile in a cave. Listen to him, as he expresses his confidence in God:

> He [God] will execute judgment for the peoples with
> equity. The LORD also will be a stronghold for the
> oppressed, a stronghold in times of trouble, and those
> who know Thy name will put their trust in Thee; for
> Thou, O LORD, hast not forsaken those who seek Thee.
> —PSALM 9:8–10, NAS

It is easy when we are outraged because of personal injustice to think that no one has ever suffered as we have. When someone suggests to us that we should seek God for a solution, we may tend to think, *That might work for others but not for me.* David shares with us that in his deepest distress, when he called on God, he found help:

> He does not forget the cry of the afflicted. Be gracious to me, O LORD; behold my affliction from those
> who hate me, Thou who dost lift me up from the gates of
> death.
> —PSALM 9:12–13, NAS

And though David chafed under the years of relentless pursuit by King Saul, which forced him to live the life of a fugitive, yet rather than avenge himself, David called on God to save him from his enemy. And God did save him, not only from Saul, but from the more terrible enemies of hatred, revenge, bitterness, and despair. And during the years he suffered such great injustice, God prepared David's heart to rule in righteousness over Israel after Saul, the apparent enemy, was destroyed. He placed his confidence in God and was not disappointed:

"Because of the devastation of the afflicted, because of the groaning of the needy, now I will arise," says the LORD; "I will set him in the safety for which he longs" (Ps. 12:5).

There are many other historical examples in the Scriptures of God's divine intervention in the lives of His people to rescue them and set them free them from injustice. The three Hebrew children who faced a fiery furnace, Joseph who was sold into slavery by his brothers and then thrown into prison because of a lie against his character, and Daniel in the lion's den—all called on God and were vindicated by His divine justice.

They learned to know God in deeper ways *because* of their unjust circumstances. And, in time, they were released from the tyranny of injustice, fulfilling their eternal destiny, which testified to the justice of God. As we bring the injustice we are suffering to God and seek Him to be our protector and avenger, He will satisfy our need for true justice. He will deepen our relationship with Him in such a way that, instead of being destroyed by injustices we have suffered, we will experience deep fulfillment in our relationship with God. And He will make our lives truly successful.

CHAPTER 9

In Search of

Success
Walking in Divine Obedience

This book of the law shall not depart from your mouth, but you shall meditate on it day and night, so that you may be careful to do according to all that is written in it; for then you will make your way prosperous, and then you will have success.
                                                    —Joshua 1:8, NAS

What does success look like? How do you measure success for your life? Are there different criteria for every person's success? Are there any common denominators for recognizing a successful person? Who or what finally determines whether or not we have succeeded in life?

Responses to these questions will be as varied as the people who answer them. Most people desire to be successful, and have defined—consciously or unconsciously—what success means for them personally. While it is easy to look at a financially successful person and label their success objectively, there is a more subjective side to success that is harder to discern. The successful CEO may have achieved his goals for his company but failed in his personal relationships or other areas of his life. And while he enjoys the apparent success of his executive position, his fellow employees may evaluate his success differently, pointing to his broken marriage, a heavy drinking problem, or an addictive "workaholism."

The proud parents of the valedictorian of her high school class may feel successful in having reared such an academic achiever. Certainly academic achievement is an objective measure of success for many. However, if their daughter's future does not involve furthering her academic achievement as she chooses motherhood or other worthwhile pursuits, these parents could feel disappointed that their daughter did not seek further success in the arena of intellectual recognition.

It is possible to be successful in some people's eyes while appearing unsuccessful in the eyes of others, according to their perception of success. And it is rare that a person would consider himself successful in every area of his life. Some pour their energies into one area in which they feel successful precisely because they feel they have failed so miserably in other aspects of living. This subjectivity of evaluating success makes many people miserable, especially if they are trying to fulfill a parent's or other significant person's definition of success for their lives. We need to find a more objective criteria for evaluating the success of our lives than the opinions of people around us.

OBEDIENCE: MOTIVATOR TO SUCCESS

God is more interested in our success than we are. He has a determination for each of us to be successful and to fulfill our personal destiny, which He ordained for us before the foundation of the world. He told Jeremiah, the prophet, "Before I formed you in the womb I knew you, and before you were born I consecrated you; I have appointed you a prophet to the nations" (Jer. 1:4, NAS). The psalmist David understood this sovereign purpose that God has for each life. He declared: "Thine eyes have seen my unformed substance; and in Thy book they were all written, the days that were ordained for me, when as yet there was not one of them" (Ps.139:16, NAS). It is

124

wonderful to think that God has a purpose of success for each of us, and He desires that we know true fulfillment in finding our personal destiny.

The Scriptures teach that if we want to enjoy true success as God defines success, we must learn to be obedient to His Word. God told Joshua, who was the successor of Moses and assigned to lead the children of Israel into the promised land, that in order to be successful he would need to pay careful attention to the law of God. God spoke to him:

> Be careful to do according to all that is written in it [the law]; for then you will make your way prosperous, and then you will have success."
> —JOSHUA 1:8, NAS

Unless we are motivated by obedience to the Word of God, we will never know true success for our lives as God intended it. It is impossible to find our personal destiny in God without submitting our lives to the will of God as revealed in the Word of God. That doesn't mean we have to perfectly understand every verse before we can expect to become successful people. But obedience to what we do understand to be God's will is necessary in order to live successfully. That means we will redefine success according to the Word of God rather than striving to fulfill our own criteria for success.

Success will look different for every believer's life who is fulfilling his personal destiny, but it will have some common denominators, which the Scriptures teach are an integral part of God's criteria for a successful life. The first of these is obedience to the revealed will of God and a heart desire to cultivate that obedience even to the denying of personal desires and ambitions. Without the motivating force of obedience to God, true success is impossible, even if we realize our personal goals in life and receive the applause of people who credit us with success. To find true heart satisfaction in the area of success requires that we understand and fulfill God's criteria for success.

The Satisfied Heart

A few years ago I was lying in bed crying brokenheartedly over my failure to find fulfillment in a classical ministry lifestyle for which I had been educated, trained, and in which I had walked for a number of years. Raised in a minister's home, my criteria for success was formed in a large part by the values esteemed in my home. Being "used of God" meant serving on a church staff, preaching and teaching the Word, praying for the sick, and bringing souls into the kingdom of God. These were high priorities in my "success paradigm" that was formed in my childhood. Besides this learned criteria for success, my own pursuit of God and consecration to obey His Word created a desire in my heart to serve Him in such a way that I would know I was pleasing Him and helping to build His church.

When it seemed that doors of ministry were closing, and I was "forced" to make a living in a "secular" vocation, I felt defeated. The enemy of my soul took advantage of my situation, making me feel like a failure because I was not in full-time ministry. The ache in my heart was unbearable at times as I continued to seek God for His purposes to be fulfilled in my life.

As I lay there crying that night, I asked God to take away any desires for success that were not of Him and to cleanse my heart of ambition for ministry, which was not part of His plan for me. In that moment, He came to me as a mother would come to tuck in a crying child. I felt Him sit down on the side of my bed, lean over me, and tenderly begin to reason with me through my tears. There was no condemnation in His voice. He said simply, "Carol, you value *ministry*. I value *obedience*."

That inexplicable thing that happens when we hear God speak a word to us brought instant peace to my heart and erased the emotional pain as if it had never existed. I felt secure in His love, recognizing that I was walking in the next step of obedience to His will that He had ordained for me. And my understanding was opened to His divine perspective of success. I was set free from my limited concept of success which had motivated me for years and caused me such pain and feeling of failure when it was not evident in my life. I knew that I had yielded to Him to obey Him and that He considered my life to be successful because of my obedience. In that quiet visitation of God to my heart, the Holy Spirit redefined success for me for the rest of my life. Whatever my task, if done in obedience to His will, it will bring me the satisfaction of knowing true success.

Claudio Freidzon, the Argentinian pastor who is credited with bringing Holy Ghost revival to His nation and to other nations, declares:

> There are no tasks that can be considered more important than others. They are all equally assigned to us by God and will be rewarded equally. Make sure you are serving God where He has placed you. What He has assigned to you is of great value to Him![19]

While it is thrilling to lead a soul to Christ and to experience the anointing of the Holy Spirit in teaching His Word, in God's eyes it is equally fulfilling to clean the bathroom and become a servant to others if He assigns us these tasks. Yet success is not only defined by God in the accomplishing of His assigned tasks, but in an even more personal way. True success is determined by the development of godly character in our lives.

CHARACTER: FRUIT OF SUCCESS

Obedience to God's Word will result in our lives reflecting the character of God. Until the church truly embraces the reality of God's Word, which teaches God's priority of holiness and godly character as the true criteria for success, we will never know true satisfaction in our life-long pursuit for success. Instead, we continually compare ourselves with each other, competing for position, recognition, and relationships that raise our sense of self-esteem. The Scriptures teach that people who continually "measure themselves by themselves, and compare themselves with themselves," are not wise (2 Cor. 10:12, NAS). We need to measure our obedience to the Word if we are to truly evaluate our success and fulfill our personal destinies.

True obedience to God produces His character in us. The fruit of the Spirit—love, joy, peace, long-suffering, gentleness, goodness, faith, meekness, temperance—will grow unhindered in our lives as we allow the Holy Spirit to continually define success for us. As we increasingly reflect His character, we will enjoy a divine sense of fulfillment when we give attention to obedience in the smallest details of our lives. As we accept this truth, every moment of every day becomes significant, every mundane task is an opportunity not only for obedience, but also for developing in us the character of God.

There is perhaps no greater thief that the enemy delights to use to rob us of contentment than our faulty concepts of success. Educated in the world's ideas of success which include materialism, academic achievement, vocational position, marital status, and stardom, we need to be cleansed of these and other worldly concepts of success in order to value and pursue godly success. Too often we transfer these worldly concepts of success into our Christian lifestyle, as I did, seeking for ministry positions and recognition through charismatic giftings in order to feel successful.

The apostle Paul admonishes us to bring every thought into captivity to the obedience of Christ (2 Cor. 10:5). As we allow our minds to be renewed by the Word of God, the Holy Spirit will redefine success for us. We will understand that loving our neighbor as ourselves, bearing one another's burdens, and rightly discerning the body of Christ are vital elements of a successful life in God. He will reveal the character of Christ in His humility, His meekness, and His servant-heart and fill our hearts with desire to reflect those qualities in our lives as well. Then whatever task or assignment He gives us to do—raising a godly family, building a business, or pastoring a church—we will bring His character to that task and make it truly successful.

In Search of *Success*

JESUS: OUR PATTERN OF SUCCESS

Jesus defined success for us through His intimate, obedient relationship with His Father. There was no task too ignoble, no cost too great, no suffering that He would avoid in order to make His obedience to His Father complete. Jesus did not tolerate disobedience anywhere He saw it, whether in the Jewish leaders or His own disciples. Disregarding the inevitable hatred of the Jewish leaders, He confronted their disobedience and made them accountable to the truth. Jesus' ultimate success depended on living His life in a way that perfectly revealed the Father to the world. His words, attitudes, and deeds were all perfectly conformed to the will of the Father. As we determine to be conformed to the life of Christ, we will be assured of experiencing true success as well.

Our success will be measured by God according to the degree of obedience in which we walk. It is not merely the task we accomplish, but the obedience that task represents that will determine our success in God. And the servant-heart attitude that performs the task reflects true obedience. God proclaimed through the prophet Isaiah, "If ye be willing and obedient, ye shall eat the good of the land" (Isa. 1:19). I am convinced that the spirit with which our obedience is accomplished is as important to our success as the task itself.

The Scriptures declare of Jesus: "Thou hast loved righteousness, and hated iniquity; therefore God, even thy God, hath anointed thee with the oil of gladness above thy fellows" (Heb. 1:9). To hate iniquity is one of our most powerful keys to living successful lives. To love righteousness is its companion key, which will focus our lives on God's priority of success: godly character. The result will be an anointing of the Holy Spirit that will bring gladness into our lives in every mundane detail and task assigned to us.

That gladness will be so attractive to the unbelievers around us that they will want to know our secret of happiness. Though we may not look outwardly successful according to their worldly standards, or even our "religious" ones, the joy we demonstrate in our lives as we seek His righteousness will draw them to us like a magnet. Success is supposed to make us happy. And they will want to know the reason for our apparent happiness.

Sin makes us miserable. While we continue in our unhappy love affair with sin, promoting ourselves and indulging our pride even in pursuit of seemingly spiritual ambitions for ministry, we will never know true success in life. Only as we place our faith in the Word of God and allow the character of God to be worked in us, choosing to love righteousness and hate iniquity, can we expect to enjoy the true satisfaction of success. It is God's desire that we be truly successful. He enables us to renounce the sin working in us and to follow hard after His righteousness. That righteousness will be revealed in our godly character—our attitudes as well as our words and actions.

FAITH FOR OBEDIENCE

Claudio Freidzon defines faith as obedience to God. He writes:

> To have faith is to obey God. It is to be filled with His faith, believe His Word, and believe everything He promises to us.[20]

Pastor Freidzon's words echo the apostle James, who declared: "Even so faith, if it hath not works, is dead, being alone. Yea, a man may say, Thou hast faith, and I have works: shew me thy faith without thy works, and I will shew thee my faith by my works" (James 2:17–18). If we have faith in God, we will obey Him. Though we may suffer pangs of death to our self life, it will be worth any amount of suffering to experience the deep contentment that comes from knowing we are pleasing God.

There is no true success without a conscious knowledge that we are living lives that can receive divine approval. Though we may satisfy our learned concept of success many times over and appear successful in the eyes of our peers, our hearts will not be satisfied unless we are walking in an intimate relationship of obedience with our Lord.

During one period of my life when the enemy was accusing me of failure, pounding me with my lack of success in ministry according to my perceived concept, I began to fast and pray that God would speak to me regarding several life issues and heart desires. Not long after an extended time of fasting and earnestly seeking God, I received a prophetic word from a well-known prophetess, who, without knowing me, spoke as if she had read my prayer journal.

Though the prophetic word addressed the specific life issues I had been praying about and birthed hope in my heart for the future, the sentence that my heart had really cried out to hear was, "You have found favor in my sight because of your obedience to Me." I cannot describe the relief, the peace, joy, and contentment that filled my heart in simply knowing that my life, while not fulfilling my concepts of success in God as I perceived it, was pleasing to God. The accusations of the enemy to the contrary were silenced, and I walked in new strength, hope, and joy. And eventually I walked into new opportunities for ministry that the Lord opened to me.

As long as we look for success in all the wrong places, including Christian service, we will be disappointed. Only when we define success as God does in His Word and allow His priority of godly character to work in our lives daily will we enjoy the true meaning of success in our life pursuits. Living in intimate relationship with Him where we can hear His voice and know that our lives are pleasing Him will bring satisfaction to our hearts that nothing else will.

As we allow the godly character of Christ in us to be manifested in our daily situations and relationships, what we *do* for God will be effective in reaping eternal rewards. To enjoy true heart success involves applying the principles of the preceding chapters to our personal lives, learning to walk in intimate relationship with God, which will result in a life of obedience to His will. That walk of obedience will inevitably bring us into fruitfulness in the kingdom of God, without which we can never know complete fulfillment.

Though being successful involves being obedient and developing godly character, there is another aspect of success in life that relates directly to fruitfulness: bringing souls into the kingdom of God. We will look at that aspect of success more closely as we study to find fulfillment in becoming fruitful in God.

CHAPTER 10

In Search of

Anointing

Bearing Fruit for Eternity

Herein is my Father glorified, that ye bear much fruit;
so shall ye be my disciples.

—John 15:8

Finding true success in God and bearing fruit in the kingdom are admittedly closely related subjects. However, we want to discuss specifically several issues relating to reproducing the life of Christ in us and in the lives of those we touch. Understanding the purpose of God to win men and women and children to Himself and the ways He accomplishes that primary goal will help us to be more effective in bearing eternal fruit in the kingdom.

Jesus declared that the Father is glorified when we bear much fruit. We will be able to satisfy the heart of our Lord to glorify the Father as we become rightly related to the Holy Spirit, who anoints our lives to that end. Without walking in the anointing of the Holy Spirit, everything we attempt will be dead works and will fail to satisfy our desire to be fruitful in the kingdom.

ANOINTING DEFINED

For many charismatic Christians, the definition of *anointing* has been limited to charismatic giftings that enable believers to give a word of prophecy or share a word of knowledge. We say a song was anointed if it brought a strong emotional response, or we say a sermon or minister was anointed if our hearts were stirred and inspired by listening to them. Though these are valid aspects of the anointing of the Holy Spirit, the true meaning of anointing portrays a much more comprehensive and beautiful picture of God's enabling power in our lives.

It is by the anointing of the Holy Spirit that we are enabled to become servants, humbling ourselves as Jesus did until we reflect the character of Christ. Through the anointing we are enabled to do the works of God that He has called us to do. And by the power of the anointing of the Holy Spirit many Christians have even endured martyrdom.

The word *anoint,* translated from Hebrew as well as Greek, literally means "to pour upon or rub on." It usually involved rubbing with or pouring on oil or a special mixture of oil and spices as in the holy anointing oil God commanded Moses to make. (See Exodus 30.) There were many ceremonial events for which God commanded His people to practice anointing. These included consecrating people and even inanimate objects to the service of God, comforting those in mourning, and establishing a memorial. Anointing was also practiced as an indication of sovereign appointment to priesthood or kingship. It was used as well in ceremonies of burial. This understanding of consecration, being set apart to the will of God, is vital to our understanding of anointing.

In the Scriptures, oil is a symbol or type of the Holy Spirit. When God required His people to anoint or be anointed with oil, He was, in type, expressing their relationship to the Holy Spirit. It is the power of the Holy Spirit in our lives that makes our consecration to God possible and enables us to accomplish the divine purposes of God. It was that consecration that enabled Jesus not only to do miracles, but also to confront the religious darkness of the Jewish leaders and to endure the agony of Calvary.

Jesus' Anointing

Jesus Himself was baptized with the Holy Spirit at His water baptism. After John baptized Jesus, the heavens opened and the Spirit of God descended upon Him as a dove. Then He was led by the Spirit into the wilderness to be tempted of the devil. And after Jesus defeated the devil in the wilderness temptation, the Scriptures declare: "And Jesus returned in the power of the Spirit into Galilee" (Luke 4:14). It is clear from the Scriptures that Jesus was personally empowered, or anointed, by the Holy Spirit to fulfill the will of God. He testified to this fact when He stood in the synagogue and read:

> The Spirit of the LORD is upon me, because he hath anointed me to preach the gospel to the poor; he hath sent me to heal the brokenhearted, to preach deliverance to the captives, and recovering of sight to the blind, to set at liberty them that are bruised, to preach the acceptable year of the LORD
>
> —LUKE 4:18–19

Matthew Henry clarifies the purpose of the anointing in Jesus' life:

> Observe first how he [Jesus] was qualified for the work: *The Spirit of the LORD is upon me*. All the gifts and graces of the Spirit were conferred upon him, not by measure, as upon other prophets, but without measure, John 3:34. Secondly, observe how he was commissioned: *Because he has anointed me, and sent me.* His extraordinary qualification amounted to a commission; his being anointed signifies both his being fitted for the undertaking and called to it. Those whom God appoints to any service he anoints for it."[21]

135

The Satisfied Heart

As we seriously consecrate our lives to God, practicing a life of surrender and yieldedness to the Holy Spirit, He will anoint us, and we can expect to bear fruit in the kingdom as Jesus declared we should. Without learning to apply the principles of consecration to God as we have discussed in our search for satisfaction, we can never hope to enjoy the anointing of God, which will make us fruitful. Every Christian is expected to bear fruit in the kingdom.

DESIRING FRUITFULNESS

Fruitfulness, as we have mentioned, involves at least three different aspects of our Christian life. It will be seen, first of all, in the development of godly character as expressed by the fruit of the spirit: love, joy, peace, long-suffering, gentleness, goodness, faith, meekness, temperance (Gal. 5:22–23). We learn to reflect the love of God to the world. The apostle Paul warned that without cultivating this divine love, even our best works become as empty and futile as a clanging cymbal. (See 1 Corinthians 13.) With that in mind, however, we are to add to our godly character the fruitfulness of doing the works of God:

> For we are his workmanship, created in Christ Jesus unto good works, which God hath before ordained that we should walk in them.
>
> —EPHESIANS 2:10

As we discussed earlier, the Lord recompenses every man according to his work, and we are to do everything as unto the Lord. Every moment of every day should be lived unto God in such a way that all we find to do will bring glory to God. As His character is worked into us and we reflect the fruit of the Spirit in our lives, we will learn to walk in the good works God Himself has ordained for us to do. And as we reveal His love to the world, we will experience the third aspect of fruitfulness: the desire to win souls to Christ.

To be fruitful in the kingdom involves our developing godly

character, walking in divinely appointed tasks, and bearing the burden of bringing souls into the kingdom. Jesus came to seek and to save the lost (Luke 19:10). As we reflect His character, we will feel His compassion for the lost. And as we do His works, we will discover His ways for successfully bringing souls into the kingdom.

ANOINTING THROUGH ABIDING

Jesus declared that in order to bear fruit we had to abide in the Vine. He is the true Vine, and His Father is the Vinedresser. (See John 15.) That abiding process results in a disciplined lifestyle that has its priority in relationship with Christ. Personal discipline is required if we are to become fruitful in the kingdom. Living in the Word and in communion with God require continual vigilance of our personal time and devotional lives. Jesus said, "He who abides in Me, and I in him, he bears much fruit; for apart from Me you can do nothing" (John 15:5, NAS).

Failure to abide in the vine not only makes fruitfulness impossible, but it will also result in our personal destruction as well. Jesus continued: "If anyone does not abide in Me, he is thrown away as a branch, and dries up; and they gather them, and cast them into the fire, and they are burned" (John 15:6, NAS). Whether your theology allows for a branch to be lost eternally or not is not the point of our discussion here. It is at least clear from Jesus' words that fruitfulness is impossible without our learning to abide in the Vine. That abiding relationship assures us that the life-giving power of the anointing of the Holy Spirit will flow into our lives and be productive unto much fruit.

Andrew Murray describes fruitfulness in this way:

> Beautiful image of the believer, abiding in Christ! He not only grows in strength, the union with the Vine becoming ever surer and firmer, he also bears fruit, yea, much fruit. He has the power to offer that to others of which they can eat and live. Amid all who surround him

he becomes like a tree of life, of which they can taste and be refreshed. He is in his circle a centre of life and of blessing, and that simply because he abides in Christ, and receives from Him the Spirit and the life of which he can impart to others. Learn thus, if you would bless others, to abide in Christ, and that if you do abide, you shall surely bless.[22]

Andrew Murray points out that fruit is not for the benefit of the branch. It is a product of the branch that refreshes and nourishes others. So a fruit-bearing tree lives not for itself, but wholly for those to whom its fruit brings refreshment and life. "And so the branch exists only and entirely for the sake of the fruit. To make glad the heart of the husbandman is its object, its safety, and its glory."[23]

THE NATURE OF THE HUSBANDMAN

As we mature in our relationship with God, the focus of our lives will shift from our personal well-being to concern for the welfare of others. Becoming fruitbearers brings this added benefit to our lives: We are delivered from the destructive power of self-centeredness in our desire to see others come into the kingdom.

Admittedly mixing metaphors at this point, in order to bear eternal fruit, we must not only become a branch that is united solidly to the Vine: we also need to have the nature of the husbandman. The priority of God's heart is the salvation of souls, restoring them to the quality of eternal life He intended for them. He is a divine husbandman, watching over His seed in the earth, the Word of God, until it brings forth much fruit. The Scriptures describe for us some of the characteristics of the divine husbandman.

Patience. The husbandman waits with *patience* for the harvest:

Be *patient* therefore, brethren, unto the coming of the LORD. Behold, the husbandman waiteth for the pre-

138

cious fruit of the earth, and hath long *patience* for it,
until he receive the early and latter rain.

—JAMES 5:7, EMPHASIS ADDED

Patience requires a strength of heart that the immature do
not possess. Jesus taught: "In your patience possess ye your
souls" (Luke 21:19). He was referring to the characteristic of
"perseverance," as it is also translated (NAS). While
endurance need not have the connotation of dejectedness or
lack of joy, it does involve a fortitude that will not give up
until it has the desired result: the eternal fruit for which it has
labored.

Waiting. An element of time is involved in the work of the
husbandman. The Scriptures declare that he waits. After the
soil is prepared and the seed is planted, the husbandman must
wait for the other elements involved in bringing for that seed
to maturity—the earth, the rains, and the sunshine. Without
these elements affecting the seed over time, there will be no
harvest.

Protecting. While he is waiting, the husbandman is vigilant
to protect the seed from destructive elements. Birds that would
try to carry the seed away before it can germinate, varmints
that would nibble on the young tender shoots that sprout, and
beasts that would trample the young plants—these all must be
guarded against, for they threaten the harvest. As we walk
with God and feel His heartbeat for the lost, we will experience the passion of Jesus when He cleansed the temple, of
whom it was written, "The zeal of thine house hath eaten me
up" (John 2:17). Our hearts will burn with desire to see the
lost saved and the church established in truth in the earth.

EVIDENCE OF ABIDING

A fervent prayer life is one of the most powerful evidences
of an abiding heart. The Scriptures teach that God is touched
with the feelings of our infirmities (Heb 4:15) and that He is
not willing that any should perish (2 Pet. 3:9). We cannot

touch the heart of God without being drawn by His compassions to intercede for the souls of lost men and women and to comfort the hurting hearts of fellow believers.

The Scriptures teach us to weep with those who weep and rejoice with those who rejoice (Rom. 12:15). As our hearts are deeply touched with the infirmities of hurting men and women, we will weep because of their pain, and we will rejoice with them in their victory over sin. Andrew Murray comments on the seriousness of doing business with God for souls:

> "If we realize the intense sacredness of a human soul
> in God's sight we will no longer romp in where angels
> fear to tread, we will pray and wait."[24]

When Jesus was praying in the garden of Gethsemane, He asked His disciples to pray and wait with Him for one hour. They could not. "And when He [Jesus] got up from prayer, He came to the disciples and found them sleeping from grief" (Luke 22:45, AMP). Fatigue was not their problem. Grief was weighing them down and they could not stay awake to watch with their suffering master.

How many times have we failed to pray and wait because we did not have the faith and understanding we needed to overcome our natural grief in a life situation. Weighed down with the burden of sadness, we were unable to pray for the victory we needed. As we grow in our relationship with our Lord, we will walk in the maturity required to pray and wait, weep with those who weep, and intercede for the souls of men. The disciples demonstrated this maturity of relationship after they were empowered by the Holy Spirit. Some even faced the trauma of personal martyrdom without recanting their faith in Christ.

INTERCEDING FOR CITIES

There is a powerful prayer movement around the world today led by people who have touched the heart of God and share His passion for the redemption of souls of entire cities and nations. They have learned the principles of abiding in the Vine and are experiencing great delivering power as they wage spiritual warfare to pull down strongholds that have held people in bondage, keeping them from coming to salvation.

John Dawson, a leader in this prayer movement, writes:

> The strongholds that bind our urban populations have power, but they are not invincible. They're vulnerable, and, if we move wisely, we can overthrow them. . . . Everything begins with worship. Everything born of God goes through a very natural process: worship, conception, gestation, travail, and birth. . . . It's in the place of thanksgiving and praise that God conceives within us His mind and heart for our city.[25]

Most of us do not live with a conscious burden for our cities. Our concerns are closer to home, either with our personal lives or our families and friends. But as potential fruitbearers in the kingdom of God, we need to know that God's heart is not only concerned for our personal situations but for our communities as well. John Dawson understands this personal perspective. He continues:

> Remember spiritual warfare begins on a personal level and escalates through increasing levels of difficulty and scope:
>
> * Personal
> * Family
> * Church life
> * Church in the city
> * National
> * International
>
> All the great victories of the church were conceived in a quiet moment of sacrificial praise, when the heart of an individual turned toward the Lord and worshipped

141

Him for His character alone. Thank God for Himself.
Thank God for the privilege of knowing Him, then thank
Him for your life and the basic provision of what is
needed.[26]

Out of our intimate relationship with God will arise a passion for the salvation of lost souls. We will be empowered by the Holy Spirit as we yield our lives to Him in worship and daily consecration. As we seek to abide in Him, we will receive the anointing of the Holy Spirit to become skilled husbandmen who will bring forth much fruit in the kingdom. That eternal fruitfulness will satisfy the desire of our hearts to see the body of Christ established in the earth. We will discover the power of unity that will ultimately satisfy our desire for complete fulfillment.

CHAPTER 11

In Search of

Unity

Realizing Complete Fulfillment

Behold how good and how pleasant it is for brethren to dwell together in unity! . . .for there the LORD commanded the blessing, even life for evermore.
—Psalm 133:1, 3

Overwhelmed by the magnificence of the Lincoln Memorial in Washington, D. C., I stood there weeping as I read my hero's words inscribed on those walls: "A house divided against itself cannot stand." President Lincoln, lamenting the terrible plight of the United States on the brink of civil war, quoted the words of Jesus as he pleaded for the preservation of the Union. President Lincoln believed that our civil war was God's judgment on this nation for having practiced slavery for two hundred years.

A DIVIDED HOUSE

Today, those of us who love God and desire to see His righteousness rule in our nation grieve as Lincoln did over our nation, which is so divided over issues of abortion, gay rights, drug abuse, violent crime, and corrupt politics. These and other national sins make us vulnerable to the judgments of God.

Disunity is not only caused by these national issues, however. The church is so divided even within denominations—much more between them—that the world must view our "smorgasbord" of religion and wonder from which "table" they should sample. Even within local church families, we find so much jostling for position through church politics that it is sometimes impossible to make the most simple decisions affecting the church without causing friction among various factions or with the church board.

And what about the family—that tight-knit unit that must live together in harmony under the same roof to warrant the merit of the name—*family*. The interdependency required between husband and wife to raise children and provide for them is constantly threatened by the independent philosophies of our day: "I'll do it my way." How many families are made of independent individuals all bent on living their own way with little time or consideration for other members of the family, quarreling over the slightest inconvenience caused by each other? It is horrifying to observe to what length members of a family have gone to compete with each other in amassing material wealth, stealing affections from other family members, or fighting over estate property.

INDEPENDENCE: VIRTUE OR VICE?

The natural state of mankind is characterized by our desire to be independent. That innate desire has been reinforced especially for Americans by our deifying of the term *independence*, making it synonymous with our democratic lifestyle. *Freedom of choice* has become the idolatrous battle cry for such ungodly pursuits as abortion, the "women's lib" movement, gay rights, and other immoral pursuits. The godless philosophy of secular humanism, our "national religion," embodies the idea of man being his own god. This idea has become the accepted norm for reasoning minds. Our school children are taught that there are no absolutes of right and wrong. Rather, they are taught to practice self-determination to move them toward their ultimate self-realization.

Unfortunately, this humanistic philosophy has insidiously contaminated the church, forming an unhealthy synthesis with our Christian philosophy of *fulfillment*. We pursue self-realization in what we consider to be a godly manner, looking for fulfillment in our own efforts and abilities that our Christian lifestyles allow. Unless we understand where true fulfillment is to be found, we as believers are doomed to the disappointment of this synthesis as much as unchurched pagans are doomed to the destructive prospects of a godless self-realization. We cannot live our lives independently from God's purposes if we hope to experience true heart satisfaction.

INDEPENDENCE EXPOSED

Seeking fulfillment through our personal independent choices is not the ultimate goal for the individual believer, if he or she wants to know true fulfillment. The ultimate realization of satisfaction for the believer will be found as he or she experiences the heart of God for His church in the earth. God desires above all that the church dwell together in *unity*— union with God, union with ourselves, and union with other believers. It is our reconciliation with God that makes the latter two possible.

To learn to live in reconciliation with God's heart and purpose for our individual lives will not only bring us contentment, it will also necessarily bring us into healthy interdependence with the body of Christ. According to the Scriptures, without realizing this interdependence within the body of Christ, we will never know true fulfillment.

There are several valid descriptions of original sin—that essence of sin that resulted in the fall of Adam and his wife and brought their separation from the presence of God. Some call it *disobedience*, which of course it was. Adam and Eve disobeyed the direct command of God by eating of the tree from which they were forbidden to eat. Others point to the root of disobedience as *pride*—wanting to be like gods, as the serpent promised they would be if they ate of the tree of the knowledge of good and evil. Pride did become the motivating force of humanity as it was of Satan, whom they chose to obey.

Dr. Fuchsia Pickett describes original sin as the sin of *independence*. She teaches that the most valuable gift given to mankind in the Creation was the power of choice. Though man and woman were created in the image of God, it was God's intent that through their obedience in making right choices, man and woman would mature in the character of God. Instead, they chose to disobey God's command, separating themselves from their relationship with Him. Choosing to live independently from God's commands, they did become a law unto themselves. [27]

The iniquity originally found in Lucifer while he was still the archangel in heaven involved pride and willful disobedience. In defiance to God Himself he declared, "I will ascend above the heights of the clouds; I will be like the most High" (Isa. 14:14). Those sins, however, ultimately revealed Satan's independence—choosing to leave the high place of authority he had been given because of his ambition to be "like the most high God." It was his *independent choice* to defy the will of God and violate the interdependence of heaven that brought his downfall, literally. That defiant independence created disunity in heaven, which God could not tolerate.

For us to be reconciled to God, Jesus showed us by example that we must forsake our independent ways and surrender our wills to fulfill the will of the Father. Jesus described His life of obedience, which reveals His interdependence with the Father: "I can do nothing of myself. I do only what I see the Father doing. (See John 5:19.) Jesus' obedience in humbling Himself (in contrast to Satan's attempt to exalt himself) resulted in complete fulfillment of the will of the Father.

UNITY: GOD'S PRIORITY

The Scriptures are clear in both Old and New Testaments

that unity takes priority over independence, beginning with the Godhead. The Father, the Son, and the Holy Spirit function in absolute union of thought and purpose. God desires unity to characterize every institution He has ordained. Beginning with the individual living in peace with God, He desires that unity characterize family, church, community, and ultimately nations.

Unity is a golden thread of truth that runs throughout Scripture, ultimately defining man's relationship to God, to himself, and to others. There can be no health or righteousness in an individual, in a family, a church, a community, or nation without learning to embrace the divine reality of unity. The psalmist understood this reality when he declared:

> Behold, how good and how pleasant it is for brethren
> to dwell together in unity! . . . for there the LORD com-
> manded the blessing, even life for evermore.
> —PSALM 133:1, 3

The power of everlasting life is released wherever God's people learn to walk in unity with each other. There is no other situation, according to the Scriptures, where we can enjoy this divine quality of life. God commands His blessings on a united people.

The apostle James declares that a double-minded man is unstable in all his ways (James 1:8). Such a man cannot receive anything from the Lord. If we determine to live independently, serving self or any other idol, we cannot expect to know the blessing of God on our lives. Jesus declared, "No man can serve two masters: for either he will hate the one, and love the other; or else he will hold to the one, and despise the other. Ye cannot serve God and mammon [riches]" (Matt. 6:24). Jesus did not say that it is undesirable to serve two masters, but rather that it is quite impossible. We will either love God or we will love mammon—we cannot give our loyalties to both. Undivided loyalty to God will bring the blessing of God on our lives.

UNITY: GOD'S DWELLING PLACE

In heaven God does not tolerate disunity caused by an independent will, mind, or desire. When disunity was created by Lucifer's independence, God cast out the cause of disunity along with all those angels who sided with him. There is no record of disunity ever existing in heaven before that incident. Neither is there any record of disunity in heaven after Lucifer's expulsion.

When Jesus taught His disciples to pray, He began by saying, "Our Father which art in heaven, hallowed be thy name. Thy kingdom come. Thy will be done in earth as it is in heaven" (Matt. 6:9–10). He taught us to ask for the will of God to be brought to earth as it is always being fulfilled in heaven. The perfect unity of heaven is the will of God for earth. Such harmony and peace are difficult to imagine for troubled human hearts that struggle with personal inner conflicts as well as conflicts in relationships.

Rev. Harold Caballeros teaches that there is only one will in the universe—the will of God. Any other manifestation of independence from the will of God is simply a usurper and counterfeit of His divine will. We will not view God as tyrannical in His "demand" for one will, if we remember that *God is love* (1 John 4:16). There is no tyranny in love; tyranny is only possible apart from love. Anything apart from the will of God violates the jurisdiction of God's love that He desires for all mankind, indeed for all of His creation. And apart from knowing the love of God, mankind is doomed to the anguish of isolation and meaningless existence lived out in impudent independence. Only as we learn to yield our wills to the will of God do we begin to enter into the wonderful life of love and fulfillment that God intended for all of mankind to enjoy.

THE FORCE OF ONE

Jesus demonstrated the power of unity in His life as He walked this earth. His absolute oneness with the will and

148

purpose of the Father gave Him access to the Holy Spirit's power without measure. The psalmist prophesied of Jesus, "Thou lovest righteousness and hatest wickedness: therefore God, thy God, hath anointed thee with the oil of gladness above thy fellows" (Ps. 45:7). All the compassion, the power to heal and do miracles that we see in Jesus' life, as well as the supernatural strength He displayed in His crucifixion was a result of the utter unity in which He lived with His Father's heart.

To such an extent was Jesus in union with the Father, that He could declare to His disciples, "He that hath seen me hath seen the Father" (John 14:9). He continued, "Believest thou not that I am in the Father, and the Father in me? The words that I speak unto you I speak not of myself: but the Father that dwelleth in me, he doeth the works. Believe me that I am in the Father, and the Father in me: or else believe me for the very works' sake" (John 14:10–11).

As awesome as this revelation of the Father may be, the very next sentence Jesus uttered is perhaps the most incredible of all: "Verily, verily, I say unto you, He that believeth on me, the works that I do shall he do also; and greater works than these shall he do; because I go unto my Father" (v. 12). Jesus intends for us to know the divine force of union with God that defeats the power of the enemy and of our independent self-life. And in knowing that reality we too will demonstrate the "force of one"—God's divine power released in the earth through the obedient life of one believer.

CORPORATE UNITY

As wonderful as the promises of God are for the life of a believer, we must remember they are fully realized in the context of God's revealed will for believers on the earth, which is His church. The Scriptures teach that Jesus is the head of the church, His body on the earth, and we are all members in particular. The analogy of the body is especially powerful because we understand that no one member of a physical body can live or function without being vitally connected to the body.

The Satisfied Heart

I am convinced that many sincere Christians who love God, read His Word, and desire to obey Him are sickly and desperately seeking fulfillment in wrong places because they do not have the revelation of the body of Christ as taught in the Scriptures. Indeed, I do not believe the church as a whole is committed to this truth. If it were we would begin to see the supernatural power of God released to the world like we have never seen it.

The apostle Paul, who gave us the analogy of the body of Christ in his epistles, also admonishes us to be "diligent to preserve the unity of the Spirit in the bond of peace" (Eph. 4:3, NAS). He teaches that the way to do that is to walk in a spirit of lowliness and meekness, with long-suffering, forbearing one another in love (v. 2). These are not optional choices for Christians who desire to know the power of God in their lives, but prerequisites for them. Where love reigns, God reigns. And in that place of unity, the Lord commands His blessing of everlasting life. (See Psalm 133.)

Charles Spurgeon, that greatest of all preachers, commented on Psalm 133:

> It [unity] is a wonder seldom seen, therefore behold it! It may be seen, for it is the characteristic of real saints . . . As to brethren in spirit, they ought to dwell together in church fellowship, and in that fellowship one essential matter is unity. We can dispense with uniformity if we possess unity: oneness of life, truth, and way; oneness in Christ Jesus; oneness of object and spirit—these we must have, or our assemblies will be synagogues of contention rather than churches of Christ.[28]

He confirms as well the source of disunity:

> How sad is it to see religion wearing a coat of divers colours; to see Christians of so many opinions, and going so many different ways! It is Satan that has sown these tares of division. He first divided men from God, and then one man from another.

I do not believe that in order to experience unity in the body of Christ, denominations have to be abolished and every believer practice the same form of church government or see eye-to-eye on every doctrine. But we have to decide to love one another and fellowship around our common understanding of the gospel in the spirit of unity in order to know the power and blessing of unity in the body of Christ. Matthew Henry described the blessing of heaven that fills Christians who determine to love each other:

> Loving people are blessed people. For they are blessed of God, and therefore blessed indeed. Those that dwell in love not only dwell in God, but do already dwell in heaven. As the perfection of love is the blessedness of heaven, so the sincerity of love is the earnest of that blessedness. Those that live in love and peace shall have the God of love and peace with them now, and they shall be with him shortly, with him for ever, in the world of endless love and peace.[29]

Jesus' high priestly prayer for His disciples, and for all who would later believe on Him, revealed His deep desire that they might be one as He is One with His Father (John 17:20–21). He prayed, "And the glory which Thou hast given Me I have given to them; that they may be one, just as We are one—v. 22, NAS). We are incapable of being united with God, with ourselves, or with others, apart from receiving the glory that Jesus had with the Father.

RESULTS OF UNITY

Besides the personal fulfillment that cannot be found without living in unity with God, with ourselves, and with others, there are other profound benefits of seeking to live in unity. Again, it is in Jesus' prayer that we understand His purpose for unity. He prayed:

> As thou hast sent me into the world, even so have I

151

also sent them into the world. And for their sakes I sanc-
tify myself, that they also might be sanctified through
the truth. Neither pray I for these alone, but for them
also which shall believe on me through their word; that
they all may be one; as thou, Father, art in me, and I in
thee, that they also may be one in us: *that the world may
believe that thou hast sent me.*
—JOHN 17:18–21, EMPHASIS ADDED

Our oneness with God not only insures our sanctification
but, in a supernatural way that I am not sure we yet understand, will cause the world to believe that Jesus was sent by
God to save the world. Jesus asked that we might be one so
that the world would believe that God sent Him. Our efforts to
evangelize may be in vain without the relationship Jesus
revealed we are to have, living in unity with Him as the Head
of the church and with His body. We would do well to place
our priorities where God does if we want to be effective in
bringing in the harvest that God has promised in these last days.

To summarize, a few of the wonderful blessings of living in
unity are:

- The blessing of the Lord and life everlasting (Ps. 133),
- Tasting the glory of God (John 17),
- Maturity in relationships (Eph. 4:13, NAS)
- Revelation of the heart of the Father (John 17),
- Power to evangelize effectively (John 17).

Every aspect of our personal fulfillment depends on our
willingness and determination to live in unity with the body of
Christ in the earth—His church. Whether it is justice we need,
peace, intimacy, or rest, we will be completely satisfied only
as we choose to acknowledge Him in all our ways and learn to
cry with the psalmist:

As for me, I will behold thy face in righteousness: I
shall be satisfied, when I awake, with thy likeness.
—PSALM 17:15

Epilogue

Have you ever seen a little girl fling herself into her father's arms with reckless abandon? She erupts with giggles as he swings her through the hair and then envelopes her in a hug. His strength and delight in her warms the hearts of those observing and brings an involuntary smile to their faces.

The love of our heavenly Father eclipses even the most beautiful of earthly relationships. Yet, in a way similar to the abandon of a child, our abandon to Him releases His strength of love to us and brings His blessing upon our lives. His love dissolves our cares and fills us with delight in a way that thrills our hearts and becomes apparent to those around us as well.

On a few occasions I have entered into the presence of God in such a way that I experienced a visual manifestation of Him. In those special times, I have always seen myself as a little, carefree girl, so trusting and content (words beggar the description of what I felt) that I knew only a supernatural presence of God could be responsible for such delight. The security of being loved by God, who knows me better than anyone, and protected by Him from all harm is a completely disarming experience.

One day after I had been praying for some time and worshiping Him, I was there, suddenly, in His presence. Jesus stood before me and I was so delighted that I immediately asked Him if I could go to tell the others (friends and family) who were seeking Him along with me. (It was unthinkable in His presence to do anything without asking Him first.)

I was so sure that this was the right thing to do, yet He seemed to ignore my request. I stood there, the little girl again who had found my best Friend, and repeated, a little more insistent this time, "Don't You want me to go tell them You are here?" I looked up into His face. Then, for the first time, and saw a sad look in His eyes and a knowing smile on His face.

Seeing my determination, He nodded quietly, and I looked back to call my friends. What I saw there was too painful to grasp all at once. There they were, heads down, stumbling around a large object that they refused to acknowledge was even in their path. They did not even hear my cries to them to look up, that I had found Him, and that they could come to Him, too.

When I looked away from them to the object that separated them from Jesus, I saw that it was a cross—more than life size —that they refused to behold, much less embrace. My first thought was, "I didn't see that cross before I found Him." Then I looked in my hand and saw that I held a small, toy cross, like those I had made in vacation Bible school, cut out of plywood and adorned with burned match sticks. Surely this cross in my hand could not be the same cross that was causing my friends to stumble.

Then I understood: The surrender of our lives to His lordship appears to us as a huge cross, a place of loss, but when embraced, it brings us into the presence of Life Himself and becomes as painless as that toy in my hand. The comparison took my breath away. After I had experienced His wonderful presence, the cross that brought death to my own will and way reverted to the insignificance of a small toy that could be tossed aside.

In that moment I understood that choosing to embrace that cross was all that was needed to bring me to this blissful place of His presence. Then I remembered the scripture that said of Jesus: "...for the joy that was set before Him, (He) endured the cross" (Heb. 12:2). I tried to explain that understanding to my friends, but they would not listen. All they saw was the cross in front of them—a place of pain and death to their own will and desires.

With deep embarrassment and humiliation I returned to Jesus without my friends, not knowing how to tell Him they would not come with me to His wonderful presence. It was unthinkable from my perspective, feeling the indescribable warmth of His love. I could hardly look at Him, but when I did I saw by the look on His face that He had known already. He continued to smile sadly, and I understood that He had not given me permission immediately to go to them because He did not want me to experience the pain that their rejection of Him caused me.

I experienced a little of His hurt love that day, along with the wonder and delight that filled my heart as I stayed in His presence. As I felt myself descending over a period of days from that awesome Presence, I sobbed for hours with the grief that not everyone would get to enjoy His love because they would not abandon themselves to His lordship. Instead, they would choose to follow the deceptions of their hearts that promise to satisfy them but do not have the power to do so. As I tearfully shared my experience with some, they were moved to make fresh surrenders to His lordship, for which I was deeply grateful

DISCOVERING DIVINE DESTINY

SATISFACTION GUARANTEED is stamped on every imaginable commodity or service that humans offer one another. It is supposed to mean that if you don't get what you expected, you can be reimbursed. That use of the term *satisfaction* only begins to express the need of the human heart for fulfillment and freedom from discontent. It is God alone who can declare from heaven, "Satisfaction guaranteed," to all of mankind, the crown of His creation, whose destiny He holds in His hand. It is absurd to think that we can experience true satisfaction without connecting to the spiritual reality of our personal destiny in God. Satisfaction comes as we discover our divine destiny.

The search for destiny starts as we seek peace through divine reconciliation and intimacy through relationship with God. As we embrace our personhood apart from others, learning to cultivate solitude in God's presence, we will enjoy a wholeness that will enhance all other relationships. Learning of Him through His Word and communing with Him in prayer will bring us into a spiritual dimension of peace and rest that we cannot find elsewhere.

Allowing ourselves to be motivated to please God alone, we will discover the delights of His divine recompense that involve much more than mere material success. He will fill us with His wisdom and teach us to embrace eternal values that will satisfy our hearts as nothing on earth can. All injustices suffered can be resolved as we allow Him to heal our hearts.

As our lives touch other seeking hearts, we will be able to influence them to abandon themselves to the wonderful love of God we are experiencing, the sense of destiny we are finding, and the fulfillment of our deepest longings that we did not dream was possible.

On our adventure to discover our divine destiny, we will find others who are doing the same and be united with them in dimensions of life that will link us eternally together in love and loyalty. This companionship of like-minded souls is one of the greatest rewards of our abandonment to our divine destiny in God. We discover true community that nurtures our spiritual growth and enables us to enjoy the synergism that results when we join together to build the kingdom of God, sharing the wonderful freedom we have found with others.

Covenant relationship with God is all that will satisfy the deepest longing of the human heart. Our spiritual destiny lies in exposing the terrible lies of the devil who still challenges today, "Hath God said?," in his attempt to malign the loving character of God. Jesus opened the way for us to return to the Father and experience His divine declaration, "Satisfaction guaranteed," over our lives. Living life surrendered to His lordship is an exciting adventure that will never end. It establishes eternity in our hearts now—and forever.

Notes

1. Blaise Pascal, quoted on "Jesus and the Intellectual" by Campus Crusade for Christ International.
2. Lloyd J. Ogilvie, *Congratulations, God Believes in You* (Waco, TX: Word Books, 1980), p. 79.
3. A. W. Tozer, *The Pursuit of God* (Harrisburg, PA: Christian Publications, 1987), p. 99.
4. A. W. Tozer, *Man the Dwelling Place of God* (Harrisburg, PA: Christian Publications:1966), pp. 160–161.
5. Oswald Chambers, *The Best from All His Books,* vol. 1, (Nashville, TN: Oliver Nelson Books, 1987), p. 314.
6. Ibid., p. 313.
7. Ibid.
8. Oswald Chambers, *The Best From All His Books,* vol. 2, (Nashville, TN: Oliver Nelson Publishers, 1989), p. 182.
9. Oswald Chambers, *The Best from All His Books,* vol. 1, (Nashville, TN: Oliver Nelson Books, 1987), p. 203.
10. Oswald Chambers, *The Best From All His Books*, vol. 2, (Nashville, TN: Oliver Nelson Publishers, 1989), p. 183.
11. Nicholas of Cusa, *The Vision of God* (New York: E. P. Dutton & Co., 1928), as quoted by A. W. Tozer in *The Pursuit of God* (Harrisburg PA: Christian Publications, 1982), p. 97.
12. A. W. Tozer, *The Pursuit of God* (Harrisburg, PA: Christian Publications, 1982) , p. 111.
13. Ibid.

14. Psalm 18:20; Psalm 62:12; Proverbs 24:12; Isaiah 62:11-12; Jeremiah 32:19; Lamentations 3:64; Matthew 16:27; Romans 2:6; Romans 6:22; Ephesians 6:8; Colossians 3:24.
15. Henry Cloud and John Townsend, *Boundaries* (Grand Rapids, MI: Zondervan Publishing House,1992), pp. 194-195.
16. Oswald Chambers, *My Utmost for His Highest* (New York: Dodd, Mead, and Co., 1935), p. 54.
17. *Webster's Ninth New Collegiate Dictionary* (Springfield, MA: Miriam Webster Inc., 1990), p. 655.
18. Francis Frangipane, *The Place of Immunity* (Cedar Rapids, IO: Arrow Publications, 1994), pp. 84-85.
19. Claudio Freidzon, *Holy Spirit, I Hunger for You* (Lake Mary, FL: Creation House, 1997), p. 71.
20. Ibid., p. 125.
21. *Matthew Henry's Commentary on the Whole Bible,* vol. 5 (New York: Fleming H. Revell, 1935), s.v, Luke 4, verses 14-30.
22. Andrew Murray, *Abide in Christ* (Old Tappan, NJ: Fleming H. Revell, year of publication unknown), p. 114.
23. Ibid.
24. Oswald Chambers, *The Best From All His Books* (Nashville, TN: Oliver Nelson Books, 1987), p. 385.
25. John Dawson, *Taking Our Cities for God* (Lake Mary, FL: Creation House, 1989), p.163.
26. Ibid., p. 169.
27. Fuchsia Pickett, *God's Dream* (Lake Mary, FL: Creation House, 1991), p. 84.
28. Charles Spurgeon, *The Treasury of David,* vol. 7 (New York: Funk & Wagnalls, 1886), p. 120-122.
29. Matthew Henry, *Commentary of the Bible,* vol. 3 (London: Fleming H. Revell, 1935), p. 745.

To inquire about availability for
speaking engagements for English or Spanish
speaking audiences, please contact:

CAROL NOE
415 Glory Road, #2
Blountville, TN 37617
(423) 323-9056
e-mail address: Carolgnoe@aol.com

Or you may call Fuchsia T. Pickett Ministries at:
1-800-398-0351

Or visit the website at fuchsiapickett.com